Paranormal Investigations:
The Cajun Ghost Hunter Chronicles

Stanley Jolet

Order this book online at www.trafford.com
or email orders@trafford.com

Most Trafford titles are also available at major online book retailers.

© Copyright 2013 Stanley Jolet.
All rights reserved. No part of this publication may be reproduced, stored in a retrieval system, or transmitted, in any form or by any means, electronic, mechanical, photocopying, recording, or otherwise, without the written prior permission of the author.

Printed in the United States of America.

ISBN: 978-1-4669-6131-9 (sc)
ISBN: 978-1-4669-6133-3 (hc)
ISBN: 978-1-4669-6132-6 (e)

Library of Congress Control Number: 2013909749

Trafford rev. 05/23/2013

 www.trafford.com

North America & international
toll-free: 1 888 232 4444 (USA & Canada)
fax: 812 355 4082

CONTENTS

I:	Prologue	1
II:	TFrere's Bed and Breakfast (Murder or Suicide?)	11
III:	Rita's Tequila House, 419 Bourbon Street	23
IV:	The Lalaurie House, 1140 Royal Street	33
V:	The Woodland Plantation (Cancer and Murder)	41
VI:	Jefferson Island	55
VII:	Madewood Plantation	67
VIII:	Laurel Valley Plantation	79
IX:	Laurel Valley Plantation and Edgar Fleeker	105
X:	Las Vegas and Vicinity	117
XI:	Cruising Europe	139
XII:	Cruising the Caribbean	151
XIII:	Patrick Drive and the Helms' Garage	167
XIV:	114 Adoue Street, Home of Hilda Wroblewski	191
XV:	The Jolet Tomb	199
XVI:	Paranormal Investigations: Epilogue	211
XVII:	Bibliography	217

PROLOGUE

Parapsychology: the study of a number of ostensibly paranormal phenomena, including telepathy, precognition, clairvoyance, psychokinesis, near-death experiences, reincarnation, and apparitional experiences.

I am a chemist. More precisely, I am a physical chemist. I specialize in the analysis of trace metals using the properties of light and electromagnetic energy based on equations developed by Max Planck. He is the world-famous physicist who had a universal constant named after him. For the rest of time, physicists and physical chemists will always use Planck's constant in the derivation of their equations. Because the techniques for metals analysis that I use utilize the properties of matter at the atomic level, I can't see the processes as they occur but have to rely on the measurements from the instruments that I use. Sources are used to excite the atoms in a sample, the atoms emit light, and the light emitted is amplified using photomultiplier tubes until a signal is recorded. I use metal standards of specific concentrations that other chemists can purchase and use to calibrate their instruments to achieve the same, exact results for the same samples.

The scientific method has five basic steps in all hard sciences. I will use a metals analysis of water as an example for each step. The first step is you state the problem as a question. For example, how much copper is in my glass of water? The second step is you state a hypothesis or an educated guess. In this case, I would guess twenty-five parts per billion. Thirdly, you list all the materials you use in your experiment. In this instance, I would use acids, beakers, a hot plate, etc., to prepare a sample of the water and an instrument called inductively coupled argon plasma to analyze my sample. In the fourth step, you list the step-by-step procedures to perform the experiment or analysis. For this

Paranormal Investigations: The Cajun Ghost Hunter Chronicles

example, I would use Method 200.7 in the EPA's *Chemical Analysis of Waters and Wastewaters*. Lastly, in the fifth step, you state the results of your experiment. Let's say I was correct in my guess and the result was twenty-five parts per billion as recorded by the plasma. To prove that the hypothesis is correct and the result is reproducible, I can give the sample to another metals chemist, and he should be able to follow the five steps above using another inductively coupled argon plasma to produce the same result.

Research of the paranormal cannot be verified or quantified using the scientific method. Another person cannot take the same or similar instrumentation that I use for my investigations, go to the same sites that I have investigated, and produce the same evidence. Hence, parapsychology and the methods used to investigate the paranormal have to be classified as a pseudoscience due to this lack of reproducibility based on the scientific method. This is why this book became an individual's spiritual journey—because it was personal and enlightening. I have had many epiphanies in the two years that I gathered the evidence for this book. If it was intellectual and scientific, then what has happened to me could be experienced by many. We could collaborate on the results we each obtained and verify how close the results are to each other. No one else can do the things that I did in producing this book since they can't go to the places that I've been and reproduce the evidence that I have presented in these chapters.

My interest in the paranormal began as a child when I received a board game for Christmas called Kreskin's ESP. It had a pendulum that swung as you held it in your hand while you asked questions, and the pendulum would swing to different answers on a board. It also had cards to test your ability to determine what was on the cards without seeing them as questions were asked. After playing this game, I was always fascinated with the terms of parapsychology, such as extrasensory perception, clairvoyance, precognition, and psychokinesis.

My dad was born and raised on Fortieth Street in New York City in Hell's Kitchen. He told me stories of when he was growing up and

Paranormal Investigations: The Cajun Ghost Hunter Chronicles

living in these various apartments that were haunted. One of the apartments had a closet that if you stood in there at night, the hairs on the back of your head would stand on end. The story was that this couple was engaged and the girl broke it off, so the boy killed her, dragged her, and hung her in the closet. In another apartment that they lived, there was a man you could see smoking a cigar and sitting on the couch in the living room from the kitchen. When you would go into the room, no one would be there, and you could smell the cigar smoke.

They moved into another apartment, and when he came home one day, his mom had a priest over to bless and exorcise a rocking chair that wouldn't stop rocking. Once there was a tricycle in the kitchen that started moving and traveled completely around the kitchen table only to end up at the same spot where it started. He told me that they moved out of the apartment when the spirit got destructive and pulled the dishes out of the cupboards, crashing them onto the kitchen floor. Unfortunately, my father died in 1998, so I can't verify these stories as I'm writing this book. I wish he were here so I could amaze him with the fascinating evidence that I have gathered, which brings me to my mother!

My mother, Hilda Jolet Wroblewski, was born and raised along the bayou in South Louisiana in a place called Bayou Cane. It was a suburb of Houma, Louisiana. She was the maverick of her family, left home to join the army, was trained by the nuns of the Daughters of Charity as a nurse at Hotel Dieu in New Orleans, and eventually ended up in Fort Dix, New Jersey, where she met my father. They were both lab technicians and staff sergeants. They married, my dad served in France during World War II, and they moved back to Houma after the war. They both worked for the doctors at Ellender's Clinic in Houma and raised five children, the last one being me.

Several years ago, when my mom was still living, I told her the stories of my ghostly encounters at TFrere's Bed and Breakfast in Broussard, Louisiana. She was so tickled with them that whenever I told her I was going spend the night in Broussard on business, she would tell my

5

Paranormal Investigations: The Cajun Ghost Hunter Chronicles

sister that I was going to spend the night with my girlfriend Amelie, the spirit that haunts TFrere's. She was so enthralled with my testimony of my encounters with the spirit of Amelie that she told me that when she died, she was going to come back to haunt me. In my mother's last days in the nursing home before she died, she had lost the ability to talk to us. She was silent when we visited her and could only look in our eyes as we talked to her.

One day when I was visiting and getting ready to leave, I used the bathroom in her room. As I was exiting the bathroom, my mother looked at me from the bed and wiggled her fingers in a wave at me, exclaiming, "Good-bye, Stanley Junior!" She then laughed her boisterous, cackling laugh, which surprised me since she had not spoken for days! It is an eerie memory that I carry with me always.

After she died in November of 2010, I grieved her loss for many months since I was very close to my mom. I was the baby of the family of five children, so you can say I was somewhat spoiled. After I watched a few episodes of one of the paranormal programs on television and saw the instruments that they were using to communicate with the spirits, I researched the availability of the devices on the Internet. When I received my company bonus in March of 2011, I decided to purchase an RT-EVP recorder produced by ITC Research so that I could try to communicate with my mother at home and at her tomb. Little did I know that I would communicate with more spirits than just her!

Several months later, I also received an IR camera as a birthday present, and the following year, I picked up a spirit box to supplement the recorder. All the evidence that I have gathered from these instruments is presented in the following chapters, most of them being EVP recordings with my RT-EVP recorder scanning in the FM mode at fifty milliseconds.

There are two main methods that can be used to record EVPs. First, one can record a session using the FM scan mode. This is similar to turning the station knob on a radio from 79 MHz. to 108 MHz. The

6

Paranormal Investigations: The Cajun Ghost Hunter Chronicles

recorder that I use changes the frequency every fifty milliseconds (one millisecond = 1/1,000 second). Hence, it scans twenty frequencies every second. If a spirit speaks words for two seconds, he is speaking over forty radio frequencies. If radio DJs were talking on these frequencies, because of the high rate of changing radio stations, this would sound like gibberish. If you capture the same voice for two seconds, then this is indicative of paranormal speech and should be documented as such. I take the WAV files produced on the recorder, download them to my computer, remove the clicks, minimize the noise, process the voice waves with filters to eliminate high and low interferences, and amplify the cleaned signals. The responses and the voices you will hear on my overlaid EVP videos will amaze you. Some may be muffled, and some may have noise, but I have done my best to process and clean them up for your enjoyment. These audio recordings are best heard with headphones or earbuds, especially on laptop computers.

When you watch a paranormal show on television, they perform their EVP sessions in the second method that I call the ambient mode. In this mode, no FM or white noise scan is used. They just turn on the recorder as if they were recording a conversation and, because of the sensitivity of the microphone, are able to hear spirit voices when they play back the recording or upload the WAV file to an audio processing program to clean the baseline noise and amplify the signal. When one captures a spirit voice using this method, it is very exciting because if we had hearing like a dog's, we could probably hear the voice without using one of these recorders. I have also captured voices on both my infrared and visible-light digital cameras because of the microphone sensitivities.

Why the TV shows do not use FM scans on their digital recorders and then process the evidence for presentation, I will never know. Maybe it is because of the white noise produced during the scans and this interferes too much with their presentation of their evidence. As you will see in my chapters, some of the longest, most intelligent responses that you will hear were captured during an FM scan. Many of them are clear, understandable speech. Others sound like many people or spirits

7

Paranormal Investigations: The Cajun Ghost Hunter Chronicles

talking at once in a singsong fashion. It is understandable that they do that because I learned that in order to help victims of head trauma rehabilitate their speech, they are first taught to express themselves by singing their words. This is because it is easier for their brains to utilize that part which is used for song and music than the part used for standard vocal speech. Spirits have to use a lot of energy to express themselves in this physical world from whatever dimension they are in, so singing their responses may allow them to use less energy to do it.

Also, my final point about FM scans is that you will find that many investigators will use a spirit box. This is a device that doesn't record the user's questions or the spirit's answers, but it scans radio frequencies at a high rate of speed and has an external speaker so that any spirits talking can be heard over the white noise. This is like my RT-EVP recorder scanning at fifty milliseconds; however, some of the spirit boxes they use only scan at two hundred milliseconds, which is four times slower. In order to document and record their spirit box session, they need to have another device like a camera or another digital recorder. Also, my RT-EVP recorder is less noisy when scanning compared to the spirit boxes, which is why in some of my videos, I have just plugged a portable external speaker into my recorder and videoed the session with my camera to capture the audio voice responses.

Each of my EVP sessions was around three minutes long. I found this to be long enough since it takes me around an hour to process the WAV files using the freeware Audacity from the Internet. I process both the forward voice waves and the reverse voice waves. Each EVP recording overlaid on the videos on my website came from a single three-minute recording. The answers to questions that I ask may have been elicited prior to the question or may have been processed from reverse speech. I have copied and pasted the responses to be presented after the questions. I have not ever taken responses from other sessions or files and pasted them together.

Paranormal Investigations: The Cajun Ghost Hunter Chronicles

Two things I have learned from processing these voices. First, spirits can answer a question prior to it being asked. For a spirit, time and space no longer exist, so they may answer the question before it is asked, or they may answer it after several questions have been asked later in the session. Either way, the answers may be intelligent and relevant to the history of the site being investigated or the question asked. Second, for some unexplainable reason, a spirit can give an intelligent response in reverse speech. On top of this statement, the reverse speech of an intelligent response in forward speech is usually also intelligent and related to the forward speech response!

I once tried in the instance where the forward and reverse speeches of a spirit were intelligent to record the forward speech myself. When I processed the resulting WAV file after reversing the voice wave, the speech was gibberish. Evidently, the phenomenon of intelligent forward and reverse speeches derived from the same wave pattern in an audio file is characteristic of spirit responses only. I repeat, only spirits can elicit intelligent reverse speech.

So using the information that I just presented, please sit back, relax, and enjoy the stories. Venture over to my webpage at http://www.cajunghosthunter.com/ to listen to the videos as you read them to get the full effect. In the beginning of my spiritual journey, it was always exciting when I captured clear, intelligent responses that let me know that I am never alone.

Stanley Jolet
April 2013

II

TFRERE'S BED AND BREAKFAST (MURDER OR SUICIDE?)

http://www.cajunghosthunter.com/EVPs_from_TFrere_s_B_B.html

I've been ghost hunting for years using cameras and digital photography at places like the Myrtles in Saint Francisville and the Castle Inn in the Garden District of New Orleans. I had only heard voices at the Myrtles and was awake when someone was jumping on my bed between my legs at the Castle Inn. I truly started to believe on my third stay at TFrere's, a bed-and-breakfast in Broussard, near Lafayette, Louisiana. Amelie, the sister of Ozeniphore Comeaux (TFrere), went to stay at her brother's house after her husband died for her year of mourning. She was pregnant and lost the child as a stillbirth. One night, Amelie was feverish and went outside to the underground cistern (well) to get a drink of water and accidentally fell in the well and drowned. The church ruled it a suicide, so Amelie was not allowed a proper burial next to her husband and stillborn child in hallowed ground. She now roams the house and grounds at TFrere's.

My wife, Barbara, and I first visited TFrere's on the Friday of the Thanksgiving weekend in 2008. We had found the B and B on the Internet, and we always looked for haunts on our weekend getaways. After reading the history of the house, we decided to perform a séance while we were there and printed out instructions off the Internet on how to perform a proper séance. We met the couple that runs the establishment, Mr. Pete and Ms. Maggie, and we were entertained in their solarium with T-juleps, hors d'oeuvres, and a video about the haunting at the house.

Paranormal Investigations: The Cajun Ghost Hunter Chronicles

That evening, we made all the necessary preparations in the room we were staying, the Mary Room. We lit candles, invoked a few prayers for protection, and performed the séance with no spiritual responses to our efforts of communication. We went to sleep and had no incidents at the house during our overnight visit.

I decided to start using the bed-and-breakfast as an overnight hotel for my business activities in the area. The first time I stayed overnight, I awoke to someone pulling on my toes. The second time, there was a rosary hanging on the bed, and I said a rosary on my knees before retiring. I awoke in the middle of the night to someone rubbing on my knees. Both incidents occurred around 3:00 AM.

The third time I stayed over, I awoke at 2:00 AM to go to the bathroom and figured nothing was going to occur. After I lay back down and was starting to doze off, something jumped on top of me, held my blankets taut on both sides as I struggled to free myself, and finally let go after about ten seconds. I jumped out of the bed, grabbed my digital camera, snapped a picture in the dark, which revealed nothing, and said, "You're good!"

Maggie and Pete, former restaurateurs who once owned and operated a restaurant in Lafayette, Louisiana, are very religious people and have wonderful antiques and artifacts demonstrating their devotions. What's interesting is that Mr. Pete told me a story about a psychology professor from LSU, Eunice, who stayed in that same room, the Leah Room. The room has the only bed original to the house, and thirteen children were born in it. The professor awoke in the middle of the night to someone pulling his toes. He thought nothing of it but a while later awoke to someone tugging on his ear. He went to roll over to go back to sleep, and someone whispered in his ear, "Finish the book."

When he arrived home, he immediately finished his book about people that have had near-death experiences. They had died, seen the light, and then were resuscitated and came back to tell about their experiences. I've attached a photo Mr. Pete took where he captured a

14

Paranormal Investigations: The Cajun Ghost Hunter Chronicles

free-floating object above his azaleas in the yard. To me, it has a halo and could be the Virgin Mary from Our Lady of the Miraculous Medal, or it could be Amelie roaming the grounds. I leave this conclusion to the readers.

^: Virgin Mary

I had developed a cordial relationship with the proprietors, making pralines and bringing them some each time I stayed over. They had a policy that if you were an early or late arrival, they would leave your house key in the mail box. In March of 2009, I had to stay over and arrived right after lunch. It was about 1:30 PM, and I emptied my pockets along with my cell phone on the nightstand near the head of the bed in the Garden Room upstairs. I planned to go work out at a nearby gym at 2:30 PM, so I decided to do some work on my computer until it was time to leave. You will soon understand why I'm stating this fact.

At 2:30 PM, I shut down my computer at my work desk, changed my clothes, picked up my keys and my cell phone off the nightstand, and proceeded to the gym. I spent the rest of the evening catching up on some work then eating and retiring for the night. The next day, I had to go to Grand Chenier, Louisiana, for some work and returned to my home in Schriever later that afternoon. When I checked my e-mail on my home computer the next day, I noticed that there was a voice message left on my computer phone. My Internet phone service automatically e-mails my voice messages to me. When I clicked on the message, I realized that the callback number was my cell phone that had called my home phone the previous day at 2:00 PM, the time that the cell phone was sitting on the nightstand at TFrere's!

I played the voice mail, and in the first couple of minutes of the recording, I could only hear what sounded like a fan motor running. This made sense to me as there is a vent on the wall that comes directly from the AC unit that is in the attic behind the walls of the Garden Room. Near the end of the recording was the first EVP that I ever captured, though I didn't know what EVPs were at the time. Someone's voice said,

Paranormal Investigations: The Cajun Ghost Hunter Chronicles

"Hey," and the sound is like what you hear if you go swimming and shout at someone underwater to try to make them hear you! It gave me chills because I knew that Amelie had drowned in the cistern, and I wondered if she was communicating with me from the grave!

‿: Hey!

I had to do some safety training in Broussard on Halloween 2011 and decided to spend the night at TFrere's. I did some EVPs but didn't capture anything of significance. That night, I awoke around 3:00 AM and decided to put my IR camera on record to see if I could capture anything during the witching hour. As I lay back down, I wasn't sure if I had pushed the record button, so I threw back the covers and got out of bed to check. As I threw them back, I captured a disembodied voice on the video who said, "Your growing doom!" I amplified the voice on the video below. I'm still not sure what he was talking about. Perhaps one day I'll figure that one out. Made me wonder if maybe I have a disease somewhere.

‿: Your Growing Doom

I had obtained my digital EVP recorder in March of 2011. In May of that year, I visited TFrere's for an overnight stay and attempted to capture some good-quality EVPs. I didn't record anything that was real clear, but I did capture this recording of a man, in a gruff, vocal whisper, saying, "Thank God for killing herself. I thank God for killing herself!" At the time, I knew that Amelie had been sort of a spinster when she moved in with her brother. She would do many things that were not part of the norm for the times, such as not wearing a bonnet on her buggy rides. Maybe he was embarrassed by her not wearing her bonnet and all her other indiscretions!

‿: Thank God for Killing Herself

Before I obtained my digital EVP recorder and my IR camera, I had a habit of taking pictures at the house, especially in the Garden Room,

16

Paranormal Investigations: The Cajun Ghost Hunter Chronicles

where I thought that the orbs that I captured in the photos were real, and I looked forward to downloading my pictures each time that I visited. Remember that vent that I mentioned earlier in reference to the ghostly phone call? Well, now I know that the vent is probably responsible for blowing dust all around the room and the orbs captured are merely dust interferences on the lens of the camera.

⌃: Orbs at TFrere's

Eventually, due to all my research in the paranormal and the excellent EVPs and IR evidence that I had captured in the Woodlands, the Laurel Valley Plantation, the Lalaurie House, and the Jolet Tomb, my investigations of TFrere's Bed and Breakfast finally came to an end after a very special and captivating final visit and investigation.

After I received my annual company bonus, I decided to add another piece of equipment to my arsenal of paranormal investigative equipment. I purchased a P-SB7 Spirit Box designed and produced by Gary Galka of ITC Research. Armed with all my high-tech tools, I was prepared for an intense investigation in the Leah Room at TFrere's, where the spirit had pulled my toes, rubbed my knees, and jumped on top of me in the middle of the night.

On May 14, 2012, I decided to spend the night as I had to work in Grand Chenier the next day. I arrived at 3:00 PM and determined from the guest list that only one other couple and I were staying in the main house that evening. They were staying in the Mary Room, which left me free to investigate the Leah Room, the 1894 Room, and the Garden Room to my heart's content.

I had always had a suspicion about the details of Amelie's death. It didn't seem possible to me that someone could fall into a cistern and drown. I had never heard of such a tragic event until I heard the story of Amelie. It seemed so sorrowful that a woman could not be buried next to her husband and child due to a suicide, so I decided that I was going to ask the pertinent questions to get to the truth of her sudden demise.

Paranormal Investigations: The Cajun Ghost Hunter Chronicles

I started my investigation in the Leah Room since it was late afternoon and I wanted to be able to speak loudly over the static of the spirit box when used. I hooked up my RT-EVP recorder and set up an FM scan at fifty milliseconds since I had recently had better luck using this recorder instead of the spirit box at Laurel Valley. I attached the recorder to an external Auxio speaker and videoed a real-time session as the output is not very strong if I record on the recorder simultaneously. Even though I couldn't process and amplify a recorded WAV file, I did get some real-time responses with sufficient volume as evidence. I produced video clips of the session instead of posting the entire session so that the reader can listen to the excerpts that were most captivating. In this first session, the spirits responded intelligently and knew my name. Using headphones, you can hear them say, "Stan is here."

Stan: What is my name?
Spirit: We know him!
Spirit: Stan is here!

$\stackrel{\frown}{}$: We Know Him

I also performed an EVP session without the speaker attached and had to wait to process the recording since I can only do so using Audacity software on my home computer. When I processed the EVP recording the next day, the discoveries that I made concerning Amelie's death were very compelling and verified my suspicions that her death wasn't a suicide. I pieced together the pertinent questions and responses and overlaid them on pictures for your listening pleasure. When I asked Amelie if TFrere had killed her based on what I had heard during a P-SB7 Spirit Box session, a spirit said that her head had been snapped repeatedly and someone named Pius had helped to dump the body.

Stan: TFrere killed you, is that what you just told me?
Spirit: Snapped her head repeatedly!
Spirit: Then he dumped me . . . got poor Pius to help him!

Paranormal Investigations: The Cajun Ghost Hunter Chronicles

⌃: Snapped Her Head

I then pulled out my P-SB7 Spirit Box and wasn't expecting too many intelligent responses. It is sometimes difficult to hear anything on the device unless you are lucky and happen to have a session where the moon is right and the spirits are active. I had never been more incorrect about the results I was to obtain.

In the first session, I asked Amelie if she was there since the spirits had recognized me in the previous RT-EVP session during the FM scan. She asked if I was Stanley, and I told her she's correct and "Hi."

Stan: Amelie, are you here?
Spirit (Amelie): Stanley?
Stan: That's right. My name is Stanley . . . Hi, Amelie!

⌃: Stanley? Hi, Amelie!

In the next session, I was going to pursue asking Amelie if she fell and drowned in the cistern. I received positive responses, but I had these spirits saying that John killed and they had been killed. I was captivated and needed to find out more details on whether it was an accident or murder!

Stan: Amelie—
Spirit: John killed!
Stan: Did you fall in the cistern and drown accidentally? Was it an accident?
Stan: You drowned. Were you scared?
Spirit: Yep!
Stan: Yes?
Spirit: Killed!

⌃: Killed!

19

Paranormal Investigations: The Cajun Ghost Hunter Chronicles

In this next video excerpt, I asked Amelie how old she was when she died, and here is the audio that was captured:

Stan: How old were you when you died?
Spirit: My neck broke!
Spirit: I certainly would imply neck broke!
Female Spirit: By chance!
Spirit: One, two, three . . . *Amelie!*

⌢: My Neck Broke!

Were the spirits letting me know that she didn't drown, that she was physically injured, and that was the root cause of her death? When I heard these responses, I decided to continue this line of questioning to see if there were more spirits that wanted to divulge the truth about her death. I then directly asked TFrere how Amelie died. A spirit replied, "Murder"; a woman then said that he beat her hard, and a spirit said that TFrere hurt her! I finally had evidence verifying the earlier EVP session that stated he snapped her head repeatedly, dumped her body, and got poor Pius to help him!

Stan: TFrere, how did Amelie die?
Spirit: Murder!
Spirit: He beat me . . . hard!
Spirit: TFrere hurt me!

⌢: Murder!

In a subsequent session, I again asked Amelie if TFrere had killed her and received another positive response along with a statement about TFrere and another person named Crystal hurting her!

Stan: Did TFrere kill you and throw you in the cistern?
Spirit: He did!
Spirit: TFrere and Crystal hurt me!

Paranormal Investigations: The Cajun Ghost Hunter Chronicles

⌒: TFrere and Crystal Hurt Me!

As an anticlimax to these startling and revealing sessions, I also had asked Amelie about her stillborn child since these sessions were being held in the Leah Room with the only bed original to the house. Thirteen people had been born in that bed. When I asked Amelie if her stillborn child had died in the bed, a spirit replied "Uh huh" and then said she wiped his butt!

Stan: Amelie, did your baby die in this bed?
Spirit: Yes.
Spirit: Uh huh!
Stan: Uh huh? Your baby died here?
Spirit: Yeah . . . Wiped his butt . . . Ooh ooh!

⌒: Wiped His Butt!

Assuming that the man's voice in the Halloween video in 2011 was Ozeniphore Comeaux, Amelie's brother, I asked him during a P-SB7 Spirit Box session what he meant by "Your growing doom." A spirit replied that he was suffering, and another said that he was John. To this day, I still don't know what he meant!

Stan: Ozeniphore, what did you mean by your growing doom?
Spirit: Spirit suffering!
Spirit: I am John.

⌒: Spirit Suffering!

I asked Amelie in one of the P-SB7 sessions if she was mad at the church for not burying her in hallowed ground next to her husband because they thought she committed suicide. A spirit replied that they weren't mad and called me an angel! I might have been called an angel because I promised Amelie that I would let the world know the facts she had told me about her death!

Paranormal Investigations: The Cajun Ghost Hunter Chronicles

Stan: Did you miss your husband after he died?

Spirit: Carry me, husband!

Stan: Amelie, are you mad at the church for not burying you next to your husband?

Spirit: I'm not mad!

Stan: You're not mad, or you are mad?

Spirit: Stan, you are an angel!

‿: I'm Not Mad! Stan, You Are an Angel!

The last item that I performed in my investigation of TFrere's Bed and Breakfast was an infrared video of me sitting on the bed performing an EVP session at 5:00 AM on May 15, 2012. I asked God to bless that place, and you can see an orb, like a teardrop, falling on the right side of the screen past my left shoulder.

‿: God Bless This Place!

Perhaps I solved the mystery of the true reasons for Amelie's death. Maybe this is pure speculation on my part and a compilation of EVPs and videos that just compounded lies from manipulative spirits playing me for a fool about the truth surrounding Amelie's death. Unfortunately, I posted these videos that you have seen on my Facebook page, and unbeknownst to me, it linked all of them to the TFrere website. On the Wednesday of the following week after the investigation, I received a voice mail on my cell phone that I had missed on that Sunday. The message was from Mr. Pete, and he was very flustered. He told me in the message that all of those postings about murder at TFrere's were upsetting him and that I needed to remove them from his website since there were grandchildren of TFrere that were still alive and they might sue him because of the lies that I was presenting. I immediately removed the postings on his website, and I'm now persona non grata at TFrere's Bed and Breakfast. I will miss them dearly.

22

III

RITA'S TEQUILA HOUSE, 419 BOURBON STREET

http://cajunghosthunter.com/EVPs_from_Rita_s.html

It was a lazy, sultry spring afternoon on a Thursday in Schriever when I decided to check my Facebook account and received a message from my niece, Susan, asking when I was going to go to the bar and grill that she manages on Bourbon Street in downtown New Orleans to perform a paranormal investigation. At Rita's Tequila House on 419 Bourbon, her kitchen manager, Nick, had just that day been going down the stairs when a shadow figure had mysteriously darted past him. It startled him so badly when he reached the bottom of the stairs that he had to sit down in a chair to recover from the shock; he was so shaken up.

I contacted Barbara, my wife and Susan's aunt, to see if she was ready to make the trip to New Orleans to visit her niece. She said she'd love to go, but Harold, her brother, wanted to go also since he hadn't visited Susan's new establishment yet. We decided that we'd drive there on Sunday. I contacted Susan and let her know that we were coming. She said that she didn't get to work until 4:00 PM, so I told her that we'd arrive around 4:30 PM so that she could get her staff lined up for the evening crowd.

We arrived on time and found a place to park off Rampart at Conti and strolled over to Bourbon Street. When we arrived at Rita's, which was just a few establishments down from the corner of Conti, we met the grill's street caller, Byron. He was dressed up in a lab coat like Morgus the Magnificent with this teased-up head of hair crying to touch the

25

Paranormal Investigations: The Cajun Ghost Hunter Chronicles

sky! I jokingly told him that he looked like Morgus and knew that the evening was going to hold some promising surprises for us all.

Susan came out and greeted us, and we proceeded inside the restaurant. The building design was in the shape of a backward L with a bar on the bottom left leg and the restaurant on the right proceeding to the back courtyard. The kitchen was on the left side of the restaurant through a swinging door. We met the kitchen manager, Nick, and Susan introduced us and let him know why we were there. We met the kitchen staff and the fry cook, Danny, who by the way serves up some of the best Mexican food this side of the Mississippi. Susan then escorted us up some steep stairs up to her office at the top on the left, and on the right was a storage room that opened up to fill the front third of the building.

I got out my RT-EVP recorder manufactured by ITC Research and performed an ambient EVP session, but due to the music and crowd noise from below and on Bourbon Street, I knew that the session was for naught due to the background disturbances. I then switched over to an FM scan at a fifty-millisecond sweep rate and had two very successful three-minute EVP sessions.

The spirits immediately said my name, and I responded that it was me.

Spirit: Stanley?
Stan: Yes, it's me. Hello!

^: Stanley? Yes, It's Me. Hello!

As a means of protection and to invoke peace with the spirits around us, I asked God to bless the premises. A voice told me to stop it. Another voice said, "God's love of you." If you listen closely, you can hear another voice overlaid on top of this one saying, "God entrusted him."

Stan: God bless this place!
Spirit: Stan, stop it!

26

Paranormal Investigations: The Cajun Ghost Hunter Chronicles

Spirit: God's love of you!
Background Spirit: God entrusted him!

^: God's Love of You!

I then proceeded to ask the spirits, "Why did you scare Nick as a shadow person yesterday?"

They responded, "Oh, oh, Nick is afraid!"

^: Oh, Oh! Nick Is Afraid!

Being on Bourbon Street in the heart of New Orleans, one of the older cities in the USA with the highest crime rate, it's not surprising that I picked up a spirit during this session who told about someone getting shot.

Spirit: Some black put a bullet through her!

^: Some Black Put a Bullet through Her!

The establishment owned a cat that they let run freely throughout the building. They even posted a sign on the upstairs door, which led to the manager's office and the storage room, stating that a killer cat was on the loose. This is the first EVP I've ever obtained that has an animal vocalizing in it. In the EVP, a spirit mentions a black cat, and then there's a meow. In the reverse speech of the same EVP, the spirit said, "Jill!" The cat meowed, then another spirit said, "Cat's out."

Spirit: Black cat.
Spirit Cat: *Meow.*
Spirit (Reverse Speech): Jill!
Spirit Cat (Reverse): *Meow.*
Spirit (Reverse): Cat's out!

^: Black Cat

27

Paranormal Investigations: The Cajun Ghost Hunter Chronicles

Susan had told us that someone had committed suicide in the storage room upstairs and that it would be the prime place to perform an EVP session. We didn't know how the individual had committed suicide, so I questioned the spirits about this incident and received a positive reply about the outcome.

Stan: How did you commit suicide?
Spirit: Chuck, curtain hanging!
Spirit: He did that . . . it killed him!
Spirit: Chuck!

^: Chuck Curtain Hanging

There was another response to my question "How did you die?" later in the same EVP session, making a statement of fact in the beginning response, but what was amazing was the spirit's response at the end, which covered over 150 frequencies and had a hint of sarcasm by calling me *ignorant*.

Stan: How did you die?
Spirit: People die!
Spirit (Reverse): Help me!
Spirit: I know . . . Derrick, they're asking. Is that ignorant?!

^: People Die! Is That Ignorant?!

As others can testify about their EVP sessions, sometimes it takes a spirit up to a minute to gather enough energy to answer a previous question. In this instance, a spirit responded to the question "How did you die?" later in the EVP, and the same spirit voice a minute after that mentioned that he thought he was dead.

Stan: How did you die?
Spirit: I was killed!
Spirit: I think I'm dead!

28

Paranormal Investigations: The Cajun Ghost Hunter Chronicles

︿: I Was Killed! I Think I'm Dead!

Also in this session, in response to the same question, I received a spirit saying he killed someone's son and then saying my name after the statement!

Stan: How did you die?
Spirit: I killed his son, Stanley!

︿: I Killed His Son, Stanley!

I then asked the spirits if they could give me a "Praise the Lord" or a "Hallelujah." Everywhere I go, I usually ask this question with a positive response. I was not disappointed as a spirit gave me a profound philosophical answer, and the reverse speech of his statement was even more so!

Stan: Can I get a "Praise the Lord" or a "Hallelujah"?
Spirit: I can praise God!
Spirit (Reverse): My faith was taught!

︿: I Can Praise God. My Faith Was Taught

After the two sessions with my RT-EVP recorder, I then pulled out my P-SB7 Spirit Box, which is also produced by ITC research. I had just purchased the instrument recently and had used it with great success at Laurel Valley Plantation. I was hoping for some good responses, especially since we were in the heart of New Orleans.

My hopes were not for naught. Since I wouldn't process the EVP using the RT-EVP recorder until the next day, I didn't know at the time how the person who committed suicide had died. I was assuming that he had shot himself since New Orleans is notorious for guns on the streets. In the beginning of the spirit box session, I was asking spirits if there was a lot of blood, but then I received this response when I asked how he committed suicide.

29

Paranormal Investigations: The Cajun Ghost Hunter Chronicles

Stan: How did you commit suicide?
Spirit: Hanging!

^: Rita's Hanging!

My niece immediately got on the phone and called the owner, Braxton, to find out how the person had died. He informed her that he had hung himself! We were surprised by the positive response, and I proceeded to start the spirit box and proceed with a line of questioning about the hanging.

Stan: I'm sorry you hung yourself. Sometimes life makes it hard, doesn't it?
Spirit One: He's choking!
Spirit Two: The sucker choked! He's dead!

^: He's Choking!

During the session, I also asked the spirits if they knew my niece's name since she worked there and was in their presence often.

Stan: What's that lady's name with the curly black hair that works here?
Spirit: That's Susan!

^: That's Susan!

Since I now knew the owner's name, I was sure that they would know him if asked.

Stan: Do y'all know Braxton?
Spirit: Yes!
Stan: Yeah?
Spirit: Looking for Braxton?!

^: Looking for Braxton!

Paranormal Investigations: The Cajun Ghost Hunter Chronicles

I knew that if I took infrared videos in the upstairs storage that I would pick up some orbs. Needless to say, I was not disappointed. Later that evening, after our stroll to the Lalaurie House, I turned off the lights in the storage room and took a few videos, and I found some orbs in several of them. I spliced the videos together for your viewing pleasure.

^: Rita's Orbs

All afternoon I had not noticed the sign on the storage room about the killer cat being loose. In my spirit box session, after I had realized what the sign on the door said, I saw the cat running around upstairs. During the spirit box session, I asked the spirits about the killer cat on the loose and if they liked their cat. They replied, "Hey, Froo Froo!" This was very shocking to me since it is the name of my pet poodle back home fifty miles away! It is amazing how spirits in another place and time can know the details about your life. This is more proof to me that spirits are timeless and nonspatial.

^: Hey, Froo Froo!

IV

THE LALAURIE HOUSE, 1140 ROYAL STREET

http://www.cajunghosthunter.com/EVPs_Lalaurie_House.html

After we spent a wonderful afternoon at Rita's, the restaurant's patrons thinned out enough for Susan to take a break and escort us to the Lalaurie House at 1140 Royal Street. I had remembered seeing a wax presentation of Madame Lalaurie torturing slaves in her attic at the Conti Wax Museum when I was a boy and was anxious to visit the site. Along the way, Susan filled us in on the history of the house, adding to what I had read on the Internet.

Dr. Louis Lalaurie and Madame Delphine Lalaurie moved into their mansion in 1832. They were both very influential Creole aristocrats, and Madame Delphine's daughters were the best dressed in the city. The interior of their mansion was lavish by anyone's standards. The house, made for grand events and occasions, had mahogany doors with hand-carved faces and flowers. The gigantic parlors were illuminated by the light of hundreds of candles in gigantic chandeliers. Guests dined from expensive European china and danced and languished on imported Oriental fabrics. Guests who were pampered by the bustling madame at these lavish parties could not stop talking about her and the attention she showered upon them. She was considered one of the most intelligent and beautiful women of the city. But this was the side of Madame Lalaurie that only friends and guests were allowed to see. There was a dark side to this Creole aristocrat.

Beneath the refined, delicate exterior was a cruel, cold, and insane woman. She was attended by dozens of slaves and was brutally cruel to them. She kept her cook chained to the fireplace in the kitchen, and

35

Paranormal Investigations: The Cajun Ghost Hunter Chronicles

others were treated much worse. The cook eventually proved to be her downfall. Neighbors had their suspicions about the treatment of the slaves as parlor maids seemed to come and go and stable boys would disappear mysteriously. One day, a neighbor heard a scream and saw Madame Lalaurie with a whip chasing her young female servant to the top of the roof where the poor girl jumped off and died from the fall. The neighbor later saw the slave girl had been buried in a shallow grave under a cypress tree in their yard. Due to the mistreatments of the slaves, party guests started to decline invitations and avoided gathering at the lavish house.

The cruelty ravaged by Madame Lalaurie came to a tragic end one day when a fire broke out in the kitchen. Rumor has it that the chained cook started the fire as he was tired of the torture and punishments from Madame Delphine. When the fire was put out, officials discovered, to their horror, naked slaves that were chained in the attic—some of them dead with body parts placed in buckets, and some of the slaves had body parts that had been severed and reattached to their bodies in awkward and grotesque positions. Others had excrement placed in their mouths with their lips sewn shut, and some women lay on tables with their stomachs slashed open and their bowels removed and wrapped around them, according to the paper at that time, the *New Orleans Bee*. They realized that these poor souls had been punished beyond reason and that Madame Lalaurie had ravaged the most insane forms of torture upon them. Supposedly, when a mob gathered outside the residence and the officials decided to arrest her, they were too late as word had it that in the middle of the night, a carriage had been spotted leaving the mansion with Madame Lalaurie in it, never to be seen again. Rumor has it that they either went back to France, lived in the forests on the north shore of Lake Pontchartrain, or sought refuge among relatives who lived down the bayous outside of the city. If you would like to read more about Madame Lalaurie and her atrocities, please visit http://www.prairieghosts.com/lalaurie.html.

We arrived at the Lalaurie House at around 8:30 PM. The sun had already set, and the gray sky was quickly turning into darkness.

Paranormal Investigations: The Cajun Ghost Hunter Chronicles

Fortunately, the number of people in the streets in this area of the quarter was very thin, which made it excellent for EVP research. I immediately started an EVP session with the RT-EVP recorder at fifty milliseconds and in the ambient mode with no FM scan. The story of the little girl being chased by Madame Lalaurie weighed heavy on my mind, and I pursued a line of questioning related to her death. After only fifteen seconds into the EVP session, I picked up a command by a spirit that was both frightening and disturbing. Could this have been Madame Lalaurie expressing her wishes for the little servant's demise?

Spirit: Destroy the little one.

⌃: Destroy the Little One

What's really captivating is that at the thirty-second mark, I picked up two spirit voices with differing views on the situation that must have unfolded before their eyes and was part of the residual event.

Spirit One: Save the little one!
Spirit Two: Let her jump off!

⌃: Save the Little One! Let Her Jump Off!

I then switched the recorder over to FM scan for a fascinating three-minute-and-thirty-second session, one of the most relevant and historical sessions of my short experience of recording EVPs. I first asked if there were any slaves walking there. They immediately let their presence be known.

Stan: Are there any slaves walking here?
Spirit: Slaves are here.

⌃: Slaves Are Here

Paranormal Investigations: The Cajun Ghost Hunter Chronicles

I also asked the little girl who committed suicide if she was walking the grounds. Perhaps her name was Christian as a spirit said that name while describing what he saw.

Stan: Is there a little girl who jumped out the window? Are you walking here?
Spirit: Christian jumped off!

^: Christian Jumped Off!

A spirit then made a statement related to the question about the little girl that was both profound and sorrowful in relation to where Madame Lalaurie put the body to rest. It's sad and tragic that she was laid to rest on the very grounds where she died.

Stan: Is there a little girl who jumped out the window? Are you walking here?
Spirit: You can't bury children like dirt!

^: You Can't Bury Children like Dirt!

I then proceeded to ask the spirits how they died and what Madame Lalaurie had done to them. The first spirit response to my question was very sad and reminded me of the display in the Conti Wax Museum. Many thanks to Jacob Krejci for the wonderful picture that the next EVPs are overlaid onto. The picture and overlay brings back the horror, the terror, and the suffering that this demon inflicted on these poor, lost souls.

Stan: How did you die?
Spirit: They killed my brother! They tortured him! Bad madame choked him!

^: They Killed My Brother!

Paranormal Investigations: The Cajun Ghost Hunter Chronicles

It was almost like they were waiting for these two questions to let me know about the death and misery that was committed and that they endured.

Stan: What did Madame Lalaurie do to you?
Spirit: Elton . . . he was killed!

⌒: Elton, He Was Killed!

Stan: What did Madame Lalaurie do to you?
Spirit: Killed Isaac . . . Clyde whipped me!

⌒: Killed Isaac . . . Clyde Whipped Me!

I then pulled out my P-SB7 Spirit Box and performed an EVP session with it. My niece, Susan, assisted in questioning the spirits about their mistreatment, and her sympathetic statements seemed to evoke responses from spirits that had suffered at the hands of Madame Delphine Lalaurie!

Susan: Did Madame Lalaurie make you brush her hair? Were you afraid to brush Madame Lalaurie's hair?
Spirit: Uh huh . . . Yeah.
Susan: Did you kill yourself because you were afraid of Madame Lalaurie?
Spirit: I was afraid of that!
Susan: Do you want Madame Lalaurie to stop hurting you?
Spirits: Yeah . . . Uh huh!
Stan: Uh huh?
Susan: I'm sorry that she was mean to you!
Stan: Too much suffering here!
Spirit: She beat me!
Stan: You were killed by Madame Lalaurie?
Spirit: Killed!
Stan: Killed?!
Susan: Were you trapped under the floorboards?

Paranormal Investigations: The Cajun Ghost Hunter Chronicles

Stan: Yeah, that's what I wanted to ask.
Spirit: She beat me!

^: She Beat Me!

I had used my Vivitar IR camera to take a video of the building to see if I could capture any orbs floating around. I did capture this one orb, and right when it passes in front of the camera, you can hear this voice that says, "Summon the dead."

^: Summon the Dead!

A ghost tour then arrived, and the tour guide proceeded to tell the tourists about the Lalaurie House and the strange, grotesque occurrences that had happened at this mansion. We left there and proceeded back to Rita's so that Susan could get back to work and we could drive back to Schriever. We all felt that we had witnessed and participated in a timeless journey back into the past of one of the most sinister and insane women of New Orleans. If ever a demon had incarnated into flesh, then Madame Delphine Lalaurie was that entity.

V

THE WOODLAND PLANTATION (CANCER AND MURDER)

http://cajunghosthunter.com/EVPs_Woodland_Plantation.html

Since I have a job in which I am required to travel frequently, I decided that I needed to find a B and B near Venice, Louisiana, where I do business and which has no hotels that I feel safe staying. When I was looking on the Internet, I found that the Woodland Plantation in West Pointe a la Hache not only filled the bill, but it was also haunted beyond my wildest dreams. Not only is the house pictured on the bottle of the popular whiskey Southern Comfort, but it has a history that involves riverboat captains, pirates, and slaves.

Built in the 1830s by one of America's first chief riverboat pilots, William Johnson, Woodland Plantation became an active sugarcane plantation. He was also a pirate along with his friend from Nova Scotia, George Bradish. They came down to the Deep Delta in the late 1700s, having worked for Juan Ronquillo. Ten years before the Louisiana Purchase, the captains together built their grand home of Magnolia Plantation, four miles south of where Woodland presently stands. Both families inhabited the house until William sold his share after forty years and started Woodland.

Erecting one of the most modern sugarcane mills of its time, Captain Johnson and his sons established a profitable, thriving sugarcane business. Even though he was busy being a pirate, a slave trader, a river pilot, a captain, and a planter, there was much more that William Johnson did. He went to New York City in the 1820s and opened a refinery and distillery there, using the sugarcane from his thriving plantations in the delta of Louisiana as the raw material. He

Paranormal Investigations: The Cajun Ghost Hunter Chronicles

accumulated as much property as possible in the city, recognizing its rapid growth. Most of his purchases were along the Hudson waterfront, giving him steamboat docking for his distillery. One of his distilleries (he supposedly owned several) was located on two crosstown blocks from Fifteenth to Sixteenth Streets between Ninth and Eleventh Avenues.

Jean Lafitte, the pirate famous for assisting General Andrew Jackson in defeating the British in the War of 1812, was also in partnership with William Johnson in the business of dealing slaves. The famous pirate, along with his first mate, Dominique You, would pirate slave ships offshore in the Gulf of Mexico and bring them up Grand Bayou, a shortcut from the gulf to Woodland. The slaves were then housed in four large two-story brick slave quarters. These slave quarters preceded Woodland until Johnson's shares of Magnolia were sold. Johnson and Bradish would pick up the slaves from their quarters and sell them up and down the Mississippi Delta. Unfortunately, Hurricane Betsy knocked down all four slave quarters in 1965.

An account of life at Woodland was produced during the Civil War at a confusing and difficult time. The Office of Negro Labor was sent to investigate conditions there. They found that Decker, the overseer who ran the plantation, was creating a "great ill feeling of discontent" that exuded much animosity toward him. The former slaves (now called laborers by the Union Army) said that they would "accept even the Devil for an overseer, if you will only remove this man!" They even begged to enlist in the Union Army because of the poor living conditions. They complained that Decker was "lecherous toward their women" and that their rations were "unfairly curtailed" by him. After the inspectors left, Decker is said to have "used seditious and insulting language" toward the Union and "harangued the Negroes, boasting of his unlimited power over them."

The above report is totally different from the one that appeared in *Old Merchants of New York* that claimed that the happy slaves had refused passage to Liberia and were able to earn enough money to

Paranormal Investigations: The Cajun Ghost Hunter Chronicles

buy their freedom but chose not to. In a postwar travelogue called *The Great South*, a very different view was published. "The Negroes are now making money rapidly with the help of their old masters," according to this account. "Each plantation has its group of white buildings, gleaming in the sun; each embellished with its long vistas of avenues, bordered with orange trees; for the orange and the sugarcane are friendly neighbors. When the steamer swings around at the wharf of such a lordly plantation as that of the 'Woodlands' of Bradish Johnson, . . . the negroes come trooping out, men and women dancing, somersaulting and shouting; and if perchance there is music on the steamer, no power can restrain the merry antics of the African."

In Bay Shore (East Islip) on the south shore of Long Island, Bradish Johnson died at his vast summer estate in 1892 at the age of eighty-one. In the *New York Times*, his obituary repeated the story from the *Old Merchants of New York* about what an enlightened slave owner he was. His mansion in New York City at Twenty-First Street between Broadway and Fifth Avenue became the home of the Lotos Club in 1877 after he had moved to New Orleans, but he still owned the building. In 1900, after a delay of seventeen years, his heirs tore down the building and built the Bradish Johnson Building, a modern office building.

The original Johnson plantation, Magnolia, rotted away a long time ago. Bradish owned other plantations, including Pointe Celeste and Belleview, which were in Plaquemines Parish along with Woodland. After Bradish's death, his heirs sold the Woodland to the Wilkinsons, who owned it until 1997. The property was bought at public auction by Claire, Jacques, and Foster Creppel, who own the Columns in the Garden District of New Orleans. It was completely renovated in 1997–1998 and opened in 1999 as a beautifully restored, nine-bedroom country inn. Hurricane Betsy helped to wash away the pain and suffering that the old slave quarters had represented on the Woodland's grounds. In 1998, Spirits Hall (circa 1880), formerly a church, was moved to the site of the old quarters and seemed to have a healing effect on the property.

45

Paranormal Investigations: The Cajun Ghost Hunter Chronicles

When Foster moved into the house and began restoration planning, his sleep was often disturbed by the sounds of loud footsteps and furniture being moved on the second floor. This continued night after night, which prevented him from restful sleep. When he looked for intruders, there was never anyone there. The noises did not seem like creaking old windows or owls. He describes the noise like there were several people up there. One night, the television outside of his room came crashing to the floor at three o'clock in the morning. Foster burst out the room only to find himself alone with the television at his feet. After three months of nightly awakenings, Foster had had enough and exclaimed, "If you wake me up one more time, I'm going to burn this whole house down!" This was apparently enough to calm the ghosts down around Foster because he has never again heard his ghostly residents.

Before the Creppels bought the property, a caretaker lived in the house for about three years. One hot, humid July day, he was cleaning in a guest room now called the Suite when he felt a cold breeze on his back and shoulders. He turned and saw three diaphanous figures of a man and two women floating ominously over him. Needless to say, he fled the house and did not return for three months.

Once, after the house was opened as a bed-and-breakfast, Foster and his friend Richard Fern had spent the day fishing. They returned and had a few drinks before retiring at 1:00 AM. He described the night as having soft moonlight glowing through the windows of the bedroom he was staying in called the Roost. He was just dozing off when something made him sit upright in his bed. He was unsure what had made him jump up wide awake with such urgency. When he looked at the end of his brass bed, he noticed a young boy about eight years old standing at the foot of his bed. He was wearing a white nightshirt, and Richard could only see his head peering over the bed frame. Richard was completely startled by this unlikely intruder and rationalized that the young boy had probably got disoriented in the large house when he went to the bathroom and had wandered into his room by mistake. The only problem with this explanation was that Richard remembered

46

Paranormal Investigations: The Cajun Ghost Hunter Chronicles

locking his bedroom door before retiring! The boy continued staring at him with sunken eyes, and Richard croaked, "Who are you?" The boy stood there silently for about forty seconds, looking at him with infernal eyes, and then slowly dissolved into thin air. Richard jumped out of bed, put on his light, and searched for the little intruder but found no one and had no explanation accounting for his nocturnal visitor.

Other guests to the plantation have spotted a man in the foyer wearing striped pants and with two women. Another woman was taking a shower, and while drying off, she noticed the door had been unlatched from the inside.

I first stayed overnight on business at the Woodland in July of 2009. As with all my stays at that time, I took a multitude of pictures looking for orbs since I was still unaware of listening for disembodied voices on tapes or digital recordings (electronic voice phenomena). I have since quit taking still shots looking for orbs due to dust contamination, especially at the old houses that I investigate. I now use infrared video photography to search for orbs.

It was getting close to suppertime, so I wanted to shower before I went to eat. I took off my clothes, got my towel and face rag, and reached into the shower stall to turn on the hot water. As I turned the handle, the four-pronged porcelain shower handle shot out from the wall, hit the back of the shower stall, and bounced onto the floor, and water started jetting out from where it was originally seated! I grabbed the handle off the floor where only one of the prongs had broke and tried to shove it back onto its seating but to no avail. Water continued to shoot out of the hole, so I immediately got onto my computer that was already turned on, googled the Woodland, and called the front-desk phone. I told the girl who answered to tell Foster to hurry to the house and turn off the water. He came upstairs after he shut the water off, and when I told him what happened, he accused me of turning the handle too hard! I was taken aback by the accusation, but I told him that I hadn't turned it hard and that it just flew off from the water pressure

Paranormal Investigations: The Cajun Ghost Hunter Chronicles

on its own. He later apologized and let me know that another similar handle had done that once before. Needless to say, I felt like some unseen force had made that handle fly off the valve like it did, and I had my suspicions about that place being truly haunted!

I first recorded EVPs at the Woodland on April 13, 2011. For my first EVP session, I performed a regular three-minute session with an FM scan at fifty milliseconds using my RT-EVP recorder that I had purchased a month before. Since I was in the Roost where Richard Fern had seen the full-body apparition of a little boy at the foot of his bed, I decided to pursue some questioning about who he was and what his relation was to the Johnson family.

Stan: Are you one of the children or grandchildren of Bradish Johnson?
Spirit: Yes!

^: Grandchildren of Bradish Johnson

I then proceeded to ask him his name.

Stan: What is your name, little boy?
Spirit: Will Safir!

^: Will Safir

After I performed this three-minute EVP session, I decided to play my clarinet and do an EVP session while playing—sort of like a snake charmer, only I was being a ghost conjurer using music as an energy source and attracting device for spirits. It worked! During this short session, I picked up voices that were concerned about a person named Will having cancer.

Spirits: We think Will has cancer!

^: We Think Will Has Cancer

48

Paranormal Investigations: The Cajun Ghost Hunter Chronicles

Spirits: Will got small . . . Will Safir!

‿: Will Got Small

Spirit: Will suffering hell. Does it feel bad?

‿: Will Suffering Hell

When I asked Will directly how he died, a spirit specifically said, "Will had cancer!"

‿: Will Had Cancer

Could there possibly have been a little boy that died from cancer and that is the reason he haunts the Roost? When they say Will got small, are they possibly referring to his poor little body being decimated by the cancer? In the second-to-the-last EVP, the spirit could either be talking about Will suffering the hell that cancer brings to everyone whose bodies are ravaged by the illness, or perhaps it's a slave spirit talking about William Johnson and the hell he is suffering because of the sins he committed by dealing and treating slaves as property and separating families. I leave this for the reader to decide.

I proceeded to find out about the slaves from the plantation. I asked if a spirit was a slave, and he laughed at me!

Stan: Were you a slave?
Spirit: Ha ha ha!

‿: Ha ha ha!

I also asked if there were any slaves walking the floors.

Stan: Are there any slaves walking these floors?
Spirit: His spirit's black!

49

Paranormal Investigations: The Cajun Ghost Hunter Chronicles

⌃: His Spirit's Black!

In July of the same year, I had visited and asked if there were any slaves. A female voice replied, "Just me!"

⌃: Just Me

I also picked up this spirit voice of a woman who said she killed her paw. She said, "I killed Paw, now he's dead!"

⌃: I Killed Paw!

What's fascinating about this EVP is that the reverse speech talks about the same thing! She says, "Help me with Paw . . . he's dead!"

⌃: Help Me with Paw!

In February of 2012, while staying overnight, I performed an ambient EVP session with no FM scan and captured this demonic scream while staying in the Captain's Quarters.

⌃: Demon Scream

In the same EVP session, I picked up a woman's voice saying, "Zack healing me."

⌃: Zack Healing Me

In April of 2011, I had picked up an EVP during an FM scan while playing my clarinet where a spirit said, "William shot Philip . . . dead in the hall!"

⌃: William Shot Philip

In February of 2012, I performed an ambient EVP and captured a spirit voice saying, "Philip's dead!" Perhaps someone named Philip had come

50

Paranormal Investigations: The Cajun Ghost Hunter Chronicles

to the house, and William Johnson had a beef with him and ended up killing him. William was a pirate, and surely all sorts of riffraff came through the halls of the Woodland Plantation.

⌒: Philip's Dead

On May 22, 2012, I performed an EVP session using the P-SB7 Spirit Box using reverse AM scan at two hundred milliseconds. Here is the text supporting the video with the pertinent sections pieced together.

Stan: Bradish Johnson, are you here?
Spirit: Here!
Stan: Will Safir, are you here?
Spirit: Will.
Stan: Will suffering hell. Does it feel bad? What hell did Will suffer? (The first question was from an EVP I captured from a spirit in the Roost, next to the Captain's Quarters, the previous year.)
Spirit: He's not dead!
Stan: How old were you when you died, Will?
Spirits: Eight . . . Nine . . . Ten.
Stan: What is the name of this house?
Spirit: Woodland!
Stan: Woodland . . . That's correct!
Stan: Scream if your master beat you.
Spirit: Choked me!
Stan: What is my name?
Spirit: Stan . . . ley!
Stan: What is your name?
Spirit: Jeff!
Stan: Hi, Jeff! How did you die?
Spirit: Sybil choked me!
Spirit: Choked me!

⌒: He's Not Dead

Paranormal Investigations: The Cajun Ghost Hunter Chronicles

A full-body apparition of a man wearing striped pants has been seen on several occasions. Many have speculated that it is the spirit of Bradish Johnson. I asked the spirits what the man's name that wears these pants is.

Stan: Who's the man walking around with the striped pants on?
Spirit: William!

⌃: William

On February 14, 2012, I stayed overnight in the Captain's Quarters. I performed an ambient EVP with no FM scan and captured a class-A EVP—that means it's one of the best EVPs that I have recorded anywhere. I asked Bradish Johnson to make his presence known, and the spirit response was very compelling and relevant to the history of the house.

Stan: Make your presence known!
Spirit: I don't feel I'm welcome here. I feel like they're going to kill me!

⌃: I Don't Feel Welcome!

Was this the spirit of Bradish or William Johnson standing in the midst of his slaves who would like to kill him for the horrors of slavery that father and son committed? Was it the voice of the spirit Philip who visited the house and, because of a transgression against one of the Johnsons, was predicting his own death? Maybe it's the lecherous overseer, Decker, and he knows the slaves would like to kill him due to the havoc he brought to their lives. Because the answer was so immediate, it may be intelligent and not residual. This—who was speaking—will always be a mystery . . . until the spirit tells me his name!

I also captured some nice IR videos of orbs in both the Roost in July 2011 and the Captain's Quarters in 2012. I pieced the videos together

Paranormal Investigations: The Cajun Ghost Hunter Chronicles

so that the reader can see them all at once. This house is definitely haunted, and I encourage anyone who has the opportunity to visit this fine establishment. The food in Spirits Hall is excellent, and you will have a pleasant stay along with some decent haunts! Just watch out for those darn four-pronged porcelain shower handles!

⌃: Orbs 7-27-11

⌃: Orbs 7-27-11 (Large Version)

⌃: Orbs 2-15-12

⌃: Orbs 2-15-12 (Large Version)

VI

JEFFERSON ISLAND

http://www.cajunghosthunter.com/EVPs_Jefferson_Island.html

I travel in Acadiana often and noticed a sign on LA 14 near Delcambre, Louisiana, that said Rip Van Winkle Gardens along with the days that the Jefferson Island café is open. I have a book, *Ghosts Along the Bayou* by Christine Word, and saw that the house and the café had a chapter in the book. After reading the chapter and doing a little research, I decided to bring Barbara for a day of good eats and ghost hunting on the twenty-five-acre property.

Born in 1829, the American actor, artist, author, and architect Joseph Jefferson built the house in 1870 atop a coastal salt dome on Lake Peigneur, and it is now listed on the National Register of Historic Places. Having been called Dupuy's Island and Miller's Island in the past, he purchased what was known as Orange Island at the time in 1869 covering 1,200 acres. He especially loved the fine hunting and fishing along with the relatively mild climate of South Louisiana for thirty-six winter respites from the stage. He was famous for playing the role of Rip Van Winkle, made famous from the Washington Irving tale, more than 4,500 times. He also owned a home in Buzzard's Bay, Massachusetts, near President Grover Cleveland's summer home. He once even had the president as his guest on Jefferson Island.

The heirs of Jefferson sold the house after his death in 1905 to John Lyle Bayless Sr. of Anchorage, Kentucky. In the late 1950s, his heir, John Bayless Jr., began developing the formal gardens that surround the home, thus establishing the Rip Van Winkle Gardens, named after its former actor owner. It was successfully listed as a national landmark

Paranormal Investigations: The Cajun Ghost Hunter Chronicles

in 1972 with the Department of the Interior and donated in 1978 to the Live Oaks Garden Foundation, a private nonprofit organization.

Being fond of the camellia from his visits with his mother to Natchez, Mississippi, while his father hunted on Avery Island, John Junior developed the gardens using large numbers of camellias in a great many varieties and made them the floral emphasis of his gardens. He won more than one thousand ribbons in the Southern states because of his work with this beautiful southern flower. A hired English horticulturist, Geoffrey Wakefield, landscaped the gardens with a beautiful mixture of camellias, azaleas, crape myrtles, and other plants in a series of interlocking gardens.

Bayless built his dream house on the edge of the lake, next to his conservatory, and planned to retire there. Unfortunately, he lived there for only nine months when disaster struck in November of 1980. A drilling rig operating above the salt dome below the lake pierced one of the giant caverns, and the water in the lake drained in a giant whirlpool that sucked in the drilling rig, and water went into the mines below.

As he witnessed the tragic events unfolding below him from the second-floor window of his dream house, Bayless knew it was time to leave when he felt the earth moving below him and immediately evacuated. When he returned, his dream house, the visitors' center, and sixty-five acres of the garden were covered by the waters of the newly expanded lake.

The gardens remained closed for the next four years, and Bayless died in 1985. The foundation that he endowed sold the property to Dr. Ron Ray and his wife, Carolyn Doerle, in 1996, and they revitalized the site by offering many ways for the public to enjoy the tradition that Bayless and the foundation started years ago. Doerle closed the property in 2001 after running the property for five years.

The gardens were sold in October 2003 to the Live Oaks Gardens Ltd, which is owned and operated by Mike and Louise Richard.

Paranormal Investigations: The Cajun Ghost Hunter Chronicles

Gardens' restoration included removal of debris and restoring the many buildings. These included the Bayless Conference Center, Café Jefferson, the Caretaker's House, the Joseph Jefferson Mansion, the Cottage, and the Servant's Quarters.

Over the years, there have been many reports of apparitions, ghosts, and other paranormal events on Jefferson Island. One Sunday *Times-Picayune* magazine cover story in 1925 came with an artist's illustration. In it, Mr. Bayless himself tells the story of when he was a child and he saw a man in a top hat leaning over his bed with one hand on the dresser, but he was floating upward into a glowing light. He said the hounds outside were howling away at the time.

There are reports of beds being wrinkled in rooms where no one has been sleeping, mosquito nets being pushed aside as if by an invisible hand, and rocking chairs rocking all by themselves. Even Mike Richard has a story about staying in the house. One night while acting as the caretaker, he woke up in the middle of the night and saw a glow up on the ceiling in the corner of the room where he was sleeping. He could hear heavy breathing coming from that direction, so he sat up, stayed real still, and watched and listened to it for the next hour.

Mike lives in a house next to the main house that he refers to as the Camp. One night, his little boy woke up and saw a man looking over the crib of his little sister. The man's feet were not touching the ground, and Mike explains that his son was seven at the time but is very realistic and not a dreamer.

A repairman named Roy Patout was working at the house one evening at dusk and saw a light on the floor in the dining room as he walked in from the hall. He thought maybe it was light from a car in the parking lot reflecting off a mirror and thought nothing of it. As he was walking away, the light followed him, so he walked to the window to see if someone was outside with a flashlight and playing a trick on him. Only his truck was in the parking lot, and no ray of sunlight was reflecting off the mirrors or windshield of his truck. When he turned to go back

Paranormal Investigations: The Cajun Ghost Hunter Chronicles

into the hall, the light was there as if it had been waiting for him. He then closed all the doors leading into the hallway so that it would be pitch dark, but the light was still there. It then got real cold. There's a Cajun saying that says that when it gets real cold, that's when the ghosts appear to the living. He dashed out of there immediately. He won't say he was terrified, but he didn't close the door on his way out!

Some of the old-timers in the vicinity think that the Cottage is haunted by a man who died there. Supposedly, he was sitting on his porch in his rocker when he died, and his body remained there for several days before he was discovered. This was at a time before the salt-mining operation, and the island was pretty isolated. One day recently, a man went to pick up the waste in the Cottage, and after the screen door shut behind him, he heard it open and close again. When he turned around, no one was there.

In 1928, there was a discovery of four brick boxes with lead covers that were discovered by a work crew digging in an area on the map known as Voodoo Land. A traiteur named Daylight, the foreman, gave the rest of the crew the day off after the discovery, and the next day, Daylight was gone along with the treasure. The coins in the boxes were supposedly treasure from Jean Lafitte and his excursions in the area. It also may have been treasure from the Civil War when the residents buried their valuables to hide them from the invading Union troops. The coins were French, English, and Mexican in origin, and Mr. Bayless was able to buy some of the coins back. Mike has some of the coins in his possession in the house.

Tour guides have heard the slamming of doors and footsteps in the upstairs rooms when they were in the house alone. One tour guide was upstairs cleaning in the Camellia Room when she looked up and saw a pair of pants like someone standing there. When she looked again, they were gone.

Two sisters, Joyce and Shirlene, worked in the Café Jefferson. They recall several bizarre activities, such as beer bottles crashing to the

60

Paranormal Investigations: The Cajun Ghost Hunter Chronicles

floor and Styrofoam cups spewing all over the room from where they were stored. Joyce fled the room when the cups started flying but returned when the activity subsided. Shirlene took a picture of five employees one evening after work that included Joyce. When the picture was developed, the picture had six people in it. Although Joyce was sitting alone, in the picture she appeared to be sitting on the lap of a man who appeared to be Spanish and wearing a goatee.

Barbara and I arrived on Jefferson Island around 11:30 AM one Sunday morning. We decided to purchase tickets to tour the grounds and the Jefferson House and then made our way to Café Jefferson for lunch. After we placed our order, I placed my RT-EVP recorder on the table set on FM scan at fifty milliseconds and performed several sessions while sitting there. There were other patrons in the restaurant at the time, but the noise contamination was minimal, and I was able to pick up the spirit voices from the white noise when I processed them the next day.

While waiting for our food, I turned the recorder on and occasionally bent over it to ask questions of any wandering spirits. I asked a question about the buried treasure that had been stolen.

Stan: Where is the buried treasure?
Spirit: Spanish Road!

⌢: Spanish Road

Needless to say, when I processed this EVP and heard the response, I immediately looked up the location of Spanish Road. There is a Spanish Lake Road less than ten miles away from Jefferson Island near New Iberia!

I then asked the spirit if he was a pirate with Jean Lafitte.

Stan: Were you a pirate with Jean Lafitte?
Spirit: Pirate seekers!

61

Paranormal Investigations: The Cajun Ghost Hunter Chronicles

⌃: Pirate Seekers

Remembering what happened to Joyce and Shirlene, I asked the spirits a question about their actions.

Stan: Why do y'all move bottles around, and why do you throw Styrofoam cups?
Spirit: Kill!

⌃: Kill!

I asked if Joseph Jefferson was present. A spirit got belligerent with me!

Stan: Is Mr. Jefferson here?
Spirit: Don't you mess with me!

⌃: Don't You Mess with Me

We finished eating and walked around the beautiful gardens. We had to wait about an hour for the tour, and about fifteen minutes before it started, we made our way to the house and waited on the porch. While waiting, I performed a few EVP sessions.

Stan: What is your name?
Spirit: Hi!

⌃: Hi!

Unfortunately, not all spirits can remember their names as time goes on and the memories from their corporeal bodies begin to fade.

Stan: What is your name?
Spirit: I don't have a clue!

⌃: I Don't Have a Clue!

62

Paranormal Investigations: The Cajun Ghost Hunter Chronicles

Barbara had been walking around the porch, and when she came up to me, I asked her about the tour, and a spirit had an opinion about the tour guide.

Stan: Are they ready to give the tour?
Spirit: Freaky manager!

^: Freaky Manager!

Although the house was built in the 1870s, I asked if any slaves were present.

Stan: Any slaves around here?
Spirit: Check around here.

^: Any Slaves around Here?

I asked a spirit if they were a slave. They were affirmative and let me know of their demise. Perhaps they felt like slaves because of the way they were treated.

Stan: Were you a slave?
Spirit: Yeah . . . Mr. Pope, he beat me!

^: Mr. Pope Beat Me!

While waiting on the porch, I performed another session, and during the session, I picked up a spirit that liked to sing! What's unique about this one is that it was two spirits talking to each other! Was this a female friend of Joseph Jefferson who likes to sing?

Spirit One: Layla like to sing!
Spirit Two: Shut up, Layla . . . Sing!
Spirit One: Above me!

^: Layla Like to Sing!

63

Paranormal Investigations: The Cajun Ghost Hunter Chronicles

I put my head up against the glass of the front door and let the spirits know that I was about to go in. They had differing opinions about our entry.

Stan: Here's your front door . . . Is anybody inside?
Spirit: Tin house.
Spirit: Glass home.
Spirit: Don't enter it!
Spirit: Enter here!

‸: Enter Here!

I let them know that we were going to walk through their house. Apparently, there was some dislike for the famous actor because they let me know what they thought of Joseph Jefferson!

Stan: We want to walk through your house.
Spirit: Jefferson is a pig!

‸: Jefferson Is a Pig!

Now, I don't know if the spirits were joking with me or maybe the famous actor had a role where he dressed up in a bunny costume.

Stan: Who lives in this house?
Spirit: A big, bad bunny lives here!

‸: A Big, Bad Bunny!

Right before we were allowed inside for the tour, I went up to the door and asked if anyone was inside. I received a woman moaning and a warning!

Stan: Anybody in here?
Spirit: *Moan* . . . Beware!

64

Paranormal Investigations: The Cajun Ghost Hunter Chronicles

⌃: Beware!

We weren't allowed to take videos or pictures during our tour of the house. I tried to hide my EVP recorder in my pants pocket while touring, but the audio was so contaminated by the tour guides' presentation that no worthwhile voices were captured.

However, when we were leaving the grounds at the end of our day, we stopped by the cottage where the man had died on the porch years before and wasn't found for a few days. I performed a short EVP session, since we were pressed for time, and captured one last good EVP emphasizing the swinelike qualities of Joseph Jefferson!

⌃: Jefferson's a Big Pig!

VII

MADEWOOD PLANTATION

http://cajunghosthunter.com/EVPs_Madewood_Plantation.html

My wife, Barbara, manages a restaurant and rarely gets off two days in a row so that we can travel somewhere for overnight stays. On the July 4 weekend of 2011, she had her usual Sunday off, so since the holiday was on a Monday, I booked us an overnight stay at Madewood. We both had wanted to stay at this bed-and-breakfast for a long time because it was so close to home and because of its architecture with the big Greek columns.

William Whitmell Hill Pugh, Alexander Franklin Pugh, and half-brother Thomas Pugh moved to Louisiana in 1818 from North Carolina and settled on Bayou Teche. In 1820, they moved to Bayou Lafourche. Alexander Franklin Pugh became part owner and manager of a number of sugar plantations in Assumption and Lafourche parishes, including Augustin, Bellevue, Boatner, and New Hope plantations. William Whitmell Hill Pugh founded Woodlawn Plantation.

Colonel Thomas Pugh built Madewood in 1840–48, reflecting his aspirations. In a grove of oaks and magnolias facing Bayou Lafourche, Madewood represents one of the finest and purest examples of the Greek Revival–style architecture in a plantation home. Together, Pugh and his architect, Henry Howard, constructed a house whose classical splendor would surpass that of the neighboring plantations. Colonel Pugh acquired several plantations in the 1830s and '40s, establishing Madewood as the manor house for the group. These plantations eventually totaled over ten thousand acres. In the first half of the nineteenth century, sugarcane production brought affluence

Paranormal Investigations: The Cajun Ghost Hunter Chronicles

and prosperity to the region. Because of the blending of its classical features with indigenous material, Madewood stands out for its architectural grandeur.

The Harold Marshall family undertook a major restoration of the home after purchasing the property in 1964, and the final touches were completed in 1978. At the time of this investigation, Keith Marshall owned and operated Madewood and the surrounding eighteen acres. The fact that Madewood survives sets it apart from the 120 plantations lost in recent decades due to neglect and is a credit to the foresight of Keith. His main challenge is how to maintain a grand old plantation house while keeping it functioning and relevant when its reason for being no longer exists.

Carrying himself with a dignified bearing, Keith is moderately tall. He grew up in New Orleans, went to Yale, and studied literature with Robert Penn Warren and Cleanth Brooks. He was later a Rhodes scholar specializing in classical music and nineteenth-century British art and society. He ran the art supply store his mother established in 1935 back in New Orleans and reviewed classical music for the *Times-Picayune*.

Marshall configured not only all the rooms in the mansion but also the carriage house located elsewhere on the property, a slave quarters moved from another plantation, plus several historic outbuildings that he had relocated to Madewood over the previous decades. The first building that he refurbished was the cottage by the family cemetery located in the back of the manor on the left amid the centuries-old live oaks. Having been converted to a slave quarters at some time, it was originally a late-eighteenth-century trappers cabin. Other buildings refurbished were an 1830 blacksmith shop, which now sits with a light dignity behind the main house, and the Charlet House, a handsome peak-roofed structure built in 1822. This house was being sold for its lumber and once stood a few miles upriver from Madewood. It now forms a sort of informal courtyard, and today the cottage sits directly

70

Paranormal Investigations: The Cajun Ghost Hunter Chronicles

behind Madewood's patio, having been fixed up to accommodate overnight guests.

In 1983, Marshall acquired Rosedale, an early-twentieth-century plantation house. He moved the structure two miles up the highway after slicing off the top of the roof so that it would pass under power lines. It now sits toward the rear of the property and had been used largely for storage, including architectural salvage accumulated over the years. Because of his love for opera instilled in him by his mother, Marshall wanted to fill Rosedale with arias rather than old lumber, so he created an orchestra pit big enough to seat eighteen musicians, built a stage flanked by salvaged columns, and opened up interior walls to improve the sight lines. After the work was completed in about six weeks, Marshall coaxed up members of the New Orleans Opera, who put on a performance of Gian Carlo Menotti's *The Medium* while accompanied by members of the Louisiana Philharmonic. The show was a hit with all 130 seats sold out. Marshall would like to make full use of Rosedale and has been talking to some locals who are interested in staging traditional Cajun dance concerts there on Friday nights.

We arrived in the middle of the afternoon on Sunday and were escorted by an old black man to the back entrance. We were greeted by the manager and shown to our room. We spent the afternoon taking pictures and performing EVPs in the house. We later had hors d'oeuvres and drinks in the old kitchen now used as a reception area a step down from the back porch and separate from the house. This room would prove to be the site of the most captivating EVP on camera I've ever captured later that evening.

As we walked through the downstairs section of the house, I performed an EVP session with the RT-EVP recorder set at fifty milliseconds for three minutes. I immediately asked Thomas Pugh, the original owner, if he was there. The response, which was processed and captured as reverse speech, wasn't too inviting to me!

Stan: Thomas Pugh, are you here?

Paranormal Investigations: The Cajun Ghost Hunter Chronicles

Spirit: We want you to come join him!

^: Come Join Him!

We captured a voice near the writing table that invited me to come and write something. They were either talking to me, or perhaps it was residual. Since they called someone handsome, I have to assume they were talking to me!

Spirit: Come and write something, handsome!

^: Come Write!

There were these voices that were captured that seemed to invite someone to eat a bowl of food, and someone subsequently exclaimed a bad reaction to the taste.

Spirit One: Have a bowl with us.
Spirit Two: That food tastes horrible!

^: Horrible Food!

There was a voice captured during the session that let me know that there is an afterlife!

Spirit: Believe eternal life!

^: Believe Eternal Life!

I asked the slaves if they worked in the cane fields. A spirit had an opinion about my education!

Stan: Did y'all work in the cane fields?
Spirit: You must be well educated!

^: Well Educated!

72

Paranormal Investigations: The Cajun Ghost Hunter Chronicles

I received this voice that cursed someone named Bridget for hurting another person.

Spirit: Goddamn it, Bridget hurt you!

‿: Bridget Hurt You!

There was a voice that requested that a person named Zack Logan be brought. Perhaps Zack was a slave and someone wanted to look at him again to determine if he was going to buy him.

Spirit: Bring him back in here . . . Bring him Zack Logan.

‿: Bring Him Zack!

We then walked over to the kitchen, which is a couple of steps down from the back porch, to conduct a brief EVP session before the evening's activities. In the kitchen were antique wares from the period, one of which was an old washtub and washboard. I used this as a trigger object for a pertinent question.

Stan: Did y'all use this to wash some clothes?
Spirit: I think it's washed up!

‿: Washed Up!

I guess they figured that the washboard was "washed up" and would never be used again.

I captured a spirit that must have seen her lover coming, or maybe she was talking about me because she said,

Spirit: There comes my honey!

‿: There Comes My Honey!

73

Paranormal Investigations: The Cajun Ghost Hunter Chronicles

We had a nice dinner with the other guests and then got directions to a Fourth of July fireworks display at Attakapas Landing. We drove there after supper and had a wonderful time watching the fireworks over the water. When we got back to the plantation, we went out to the onsite family graveyard at midnight and performed a captivating EVP session where we heard many voices of the spirits buried there.

I asked Thomas Pugh if he was happy to be with Eliza again.

Stan: Are you happy to have Eliza with you again?
Thomas: Do they have Liza screaming?

⌃: Do They Have Liza Screaming?

I wondered who he meant that they had Liza screaming. I told Barbara that perhaps he was referring to their children since Thomas died at the age of fifty-four and Eliza lived on for another thirty-three years. I researched the genealogy of the Pugh family and discovered that over the space of twenty-one years, Eliza Foley had sixteen children for Thomas! Caring for that many children would surely have any mother screaming!

We then picked up a very prolific EVP. Several people I've met in paranormal research have claimed that spirits do not speak of God or Christ. I beg to differ on this issue as I have picked up spirits talking about God many times, but this is the first EVP where they have mentioned Christ. I'm not sure who Simon is as I can't find any history on this name in the Pugh family.

Spirit One: Simon's dead!
Spirit Two: Christ is bringing him!

⌃: Christ Is Bringing Him!

Urban legend has it that a male apparition has been seen standing by the fence in the cemetery. Psychics believe this male presence was a

Paranormal Investigations: The Cajun Ghost Hunter Chronicles

slave who maintained the grounds. He serves also as a guard for the souls in the cemetery, acting as a liaison to those spirits and the living who come to the site to visit on any given day.

Stan: What's your name, black man, that's looking over this graveyard?
Spirit One: That is Howard!
Spirit Two: Howard Gene!
Spirit Three: Howard!

^: Howard Gene

He wasn't very nice to me when I asked about his presence:

Stan: Are you over here right now watching this gate, black man?
Spirit: He wants me to strike him in the head!

^: Strike Him in the Head!

I then captured this voice that spoke a couple of words of endearment to his love.

Spirit: Dear heart!

^: Dear Heart

We next heard an invitation from a spirit after I asked them if there was something they wanted to tell me.

Stan: Is there anything y'all want to tell me?
Spirit: Step into the light!

^: Step into the Light!

Next in this session, I picked up two spirits that were grieving for their grandma. I don't know if she was dying or if she was leaving.

Paranormal Investigations: The Cajun Ghost Hunter Chronicles

Spirit One: Grandma, don't go!
Sprit Two: I let her go!

^: Grandma, Don't Go!

I have to admit that this EVP has a memorable affect on me because when my father with Alzheimer's was dying from congestive heart failure in 1998 and he was in the last stages of his death, my mother cried and pleaded with him to not go! I immediately told her that she needed to let him go so that he could find peace with God and get his mind and his memories back. She succumbed to my plea and encouraged him to move on. I only hope and pray daily that what I told her is true!

Perhaps their grandma was dying and it was Eliza Foley Pugh. While in front of her tomb, I captured this clear EVP that was perhaps her loving husband, Thomas, calling her home by her God-given name of Elizabeth.

Spirit: Cometh, Elizabeth!

^: Cometh, Elizabeth

The last EVP that we captured in the graveyard may have been directed at me, or perhaps it was directed at Howard Gene, the gatekeeper who is the liaison between the spirits in the graveyard and the living visitors.

Spirit: Why'd you come in here to help me?

^: Why'd You Come in Here?

We left the graveyard and went into the kitchen off the back porch of the main plantation house. I had planned to set up my digital camera in video mode, set the small fluorescent Coleman lamp on the table, and let the video run for a while to see what we would capture. Little did I

Paranormal Investigations: The Cajun Ghost Hunter Chronicles

know at the time that the sound portion of the video would be the most intriguing item ever captured on the camera.

After I set the camera up and pressed the record button, at the forty-three-second mark of the video, I picked up this wonderful, full-bodied woman's voice that wasn't Barbara's. Then at the 1:13-second mark of the video, I captured the same woman's voice, and what she said must have been residual. This voice is the purest, most wonderful EVP that I have ever captured. I copied and pasted the videos together so that the reader can hear the two phrases together.

Spirit: Moving like God! Choose all their slaves!

^: Moving like God!

All in all, it was a wonderful stay at Madewood with fireworks for the Fourth of July at Attakapas Landing and some glorious EVP sessions in the main house, the graveyard, and the kitchen. It is a wonderful feeling to not only stay at a place where you feel like you've stepped back in time but also hear the voices from the past giving you a glimpse of what the trials and tribulations of their lives were truly like. A paranormal experience such as this is not only spiritual; it's truly an epiphany that our time and space can truly merge the past with the present.

VIII

LAUREL VALLEY PLANTATION

http://cajunghosthunter.com/EVPs_Laurel_Valley_I.php

http://cajunghosthunter.com/EVPs_Laurel_Valley_II.html

http://cajunghosthunter.com/EVPs_Laurel_Valley_III.html

Once I received my RT-EVP recorder in March of 2011, I was anxious to try it out at a location other than my house. I'm not saying that my house is inactive, but I wanted to go somewhere where life had left its imprint on the land and the spirits would be abundant. I didn't have to look far because ten miles from my house, there is a sugarcane plantation called Laurel Valley. I remember driving down this long road off Highway 308 near Thibodaux when I was a teenager. There is one row of slave houses along the right side of the road and multiple rows of slave quarters going back into the field on the left. The area is now behind barbed wire, and visitors are no longer allowed in the houses due to aging and the state of disrepair.

The land that Laurel Plantation exists upon originally belonged to Etienne Boudreaux as it was given to him in a land grant in 1783. It is the largest surviving sugar plantation still standing in the South today. The original village included over 105 structures. Over sixty existing buildings include a schoolhouse, a dilapidated sugar mill, a store, and a blacksmith shop among other numerous slave homes and outhouses. The main plantation house was burned down by Union soldiers. Slowly crumbling, the old sugar mill is a shell of its original structure. In 1832, the Boudreaux family sold their land to Joseph W. Tucker for a mere $34. He expanded the plantation to include 3,200 acres. He owned nearby land and farmed his land using slaves.

By 1850, he had 162 slaves on Laurel Valley Plantation. Tucker built the mill in 1844, introduced sugar, and utilized his slave labor for

Paranormal Investigations: The Cajun Ghost Hunter Chronicles

grinding and maintenance. Slaves lived in a nodal block development in the middle of the plantation around the mill, approximately 1.8 miles from Bayou Lafourche. This made it extremely difficult to maintain contact with traffic along the Bayou. Slaves who caused trouble were shipped off to a sawmill.

After his death on July 9, 1852, from cholera, his sons, Joseph Pennington and William Pleasant, tried to maintain the property. The government's Second Confiscation Act during the Civil War resulted in a raid on the plantation during the spring of 1863. Sugar and molasses were taken, and numerous slaves left the plantation, joining the Union Army. Sugar plantations suffered as a result of the war: 1,302 sugar plantations were active in 1860, and only 180 were operating in 1865. Laurel Valley came under the control of carpetbaggers until 1867 when Tucker's son William Pleasant regained control. Joseph Pennington took over management of the property in 1869. Being from Mississippi, the Tucker boys eventually abandoned the plantation and joined friends in Vicksburg.

After the Civil War, the plantation passed into the hands of Burch Wormald of New Orleans, who expanded the mill and introduced a dummy railroad system to assist with the cane harvest. Also, there was the introduction of new labor arrangements, sharecropping, and tenancy. Increasingly, workers found themselves being paid for a crop they produced rather than labor performed. At the heart of these arrangements was the concept of consolidation. The mills focused on grinding cane and increasing their efficiency, thus creating the central mill complex. This resulted in the number of mills declining over the next several decades.

Economic relationships were also affected, resulting in debt peonage, convict labor, and the crop lien. In the 1870s, the village would soon change hands again. It was sold to Zuberbier & Behan of Lafourche Parish, and they too would soon sell the plantation village.

Paranormal Investigations: The Cajun Ghost Hunter Chronicles

During the 1880s, the sugar parishes of South Louisiana witnessed an effort by the Knights of Labor to organize sugarcane workers. In 1886, the Knights established their contacts with workers, and in 1887, they presented the sugar producers with their demands: What they wanted was $15 a month and a ten-cent increase in overtime pay from fifty to sixty cents. Plus, they wanted to be paid in species rather than plantation money. On November 1, 1887, they refused to go to work, and over the next twenty-one days, planters evicted the workers for refusing to work. The state militia arrived in Thibodaux, assisting with the evictions, and generally maintained order. Under the threat of a Negro army coming to Thibodaux, the local law enforcement officials deputized members of the militia. On November 22, the workers shot two local deputies, precipitating a shoot-out between local officials and the workers. At least eight workers were killed, breaking the strike. Not until the 1950s would workers attempt to join a union again.

On January 12, 1893, Laurel Valley Plantation Village was again sold at a public auction, being bought by J. W. Lepine and Frank Barker. By this time, the plantation was a total of 3,023 acres. Frank Barker died in 1903, leaving the sole owner as Lepine. In 1915, Mr. J. W. Lepine owned and operated Laurel Valley and invented a tractor that enabled him to plant faster than by using mules. After the death of J. W. Lepine, his son, J. Wilson Lepine Jr., took over the management of the plantation. The downfall of the sugar plantations in the South began with the Depression, and it wasn't until the 1950s that Laurel Valley was put back in full order.

Laurel Valley Village is a nonprofit group that is dedicated to preserving the plantation's built heritage. It is a volunteer group that is staffed by local residents, and there are no paid staff members. They operate a store that sells crafts made locally and conduct two festivals a year: the third Sunday in October and the last Sunday in April. At their festivals are featured local arts and crafts, antique machinery, Civil War reenactors, and food.

Paranormal Investigations: The Cajun Ghost Hunter Chronicles

In a 2005 article in the *Nicholls Worth*, the newspaper of Nicholls State University, the local college in Thibodaux, rumors had it that the village is haunted, though the general manager of Laurel Valley at the time, Jerry McKee, disagreed. McKee had worked at the plantation for thirty-one years. "I have probably spent more time walking around and inside the complex at night than anybody alive," McKee said. McKee said raccoons, possums, coyotes, deer, and other creatures visit, but no ghosts. He said anytime you get a bunch of old buildings together, stories will be created and passed around.

Ruth Himel, one of many volunteer workers at Laurel Valley, also disagreed with the haunting stories. "If you're a believer, you would believe all of that spooky stuff people tell you," Himel said. "But I'm a skeptic. A ghost would have to appear right in front of me for me to believe it." Himel said a few workers, especially one who is very superstitious, claim that there are ghosts on the highway. Himel told them that they aren't ghosts but the mist coming up off the bayou. "If that's what they believe, you can't make them not believe," Himel said.

McKee said the remains of the village seem like a ghost town because of the abandoned buildings. Not all the buildings are abandoned; some are occupied.

Laurel Valley has a cattle operation in addition to the sugarcane operation. Sometimes when they wean calves from the mothers, they are corralled up close to the buildings. They will bawl and shriek. People have said they sound like human beings in distress.

People who believe the haunting stories attempt to experience it for themselves, trespassing on the property at night by crawling under the fence. If they are caught on the property after hours without permission, and especially if they enter the buildings, "we call the sheriff and we prosecute," McKee said.

Paranormal Investigations: The Cajun Ghost Hunter Chronicles

Needless to say, I have always stayed on this side of the fence during my investigations. Unlike Ms. Himel and Mr. McKee, I can admit that Laurel Valley is very haunted, and the disembodied voices along with the EVPs captured have been truly amazing for me.

After I obtained my RT-EVP recorder, the first time that I visited Laurel Valley Slave Quarters was on May 21, 2011, the day that Harold Camping, a former civil engineer and current president of *Family Radio,* had predicted that the Rapture would occur. I went there with my son Philip, who is an Iraqi Freedom war veteran with 100 percent disability from PTSD. In my first EVP session using an FM scan at fifty milliseconds, I captured this spirit who was adamant about meeting me later that day.

Spirit: Stanley, meet me back here at six forty.

‸: Stanley, Meet Me

When I processed the EVP session later that evening and heard this spirit's voice so clearly saying my name, it made me wonder if I was supposed to meet him to participate in the Rapture that was to occur at six o'clock! Of course, I really don't believe in all this talk about the end of times and the world, but it did raise my curiosity.

In the same session, I captured these voices that were filled with hate and that mentioned killing people. Who is Spirit Four, and why did he want to kill them?

Spirit One: What is it?
Spirit Two: Don't help 'em! Hit them!
Spirit Three: We know them, but we don't like them!
Spirit Four: Kill them!
Spirit Five: And she'll be dead!

‸: Kill Them

Paranormal Investigations: The Cajun Ghost Hunter Chronicles

During a different session on the same day, I captured these EVPs talking about someone named Gordon that was killed and is dead and another voice that says that Colt killed him by the church. Either someone named Colt killed him, or maybe he was killed by a Colt .45. Not sure if these EVPs are related.

Spirit One: Look, Gordon's dead . . . killed!
Spirit Two: Colt killed me by church!

⌃: Gordon's Dead

In this session, there is a spirit that makes a meowing sound and then says that it's Wall's pig. Another spirit then says that it's a pig. Throughout this chapter, I will be highlighting some spirits' residual statements so you, the reader, can time travel and get a feel for what it was like to live on a farm in South Louisiana.

Spirit One: *Meow* . . . Wall's pig.
Spirit Two: It's a pig!

⌃: It's a Pig

Subsequently, there was a spirit that tells his friend Roland to look at the Lord, and another tells someone named Chloe to not do so. As I stated previously, many people who perform EVPs have never heard mention of God or Jesus Christ in their sessions, which makes this capture even more profound.

Spirit One: Roland, look at the Lord!
Spirit Two: Don't, Chloe!

⌃: Look at the Lord

Philip and I went back a week later to perform some more sessions in the slave quarters. In the first session, I picked up this fascinating EVP, almost like it was a glimpse back in time with someone listening

86

Paranormal Investigations: The Cajun Ghost Hunter Chronicles

to a radio station that was announcing that American soldiers had just bombed Japan. A little while later, I captured another somber spirit that said our soldiers are forgotten. It sounds like the original announcer! In my family, with all the military history from both my parents down to my brother and my sons, soldiers will never be forgotten.

Spirit One: Soldiers have just bombed Japan!
Spirit Two: Your soldiers are forgotten!

^: Soldiers Are Forgotten

On June 4, 2011, Philip and I returned to Laurel Valley. It seemed like I was going to make this a weekly ritual since Barbara worked on Saturday evenings, leaving me plenty of time to gather and process data. We captured an EVP on this day that expressed the reason for my weekly researches.

Spirit One: A ghost!
Spirit Two: Dig it!
Spirit Three: Dig it!

^: A Ghost

As I was performing the EVP, Philip walked down the road away from the slave quarters and toward the office. He was heavily medicated because of his PTSD, and perhaps the spirits picked up on his sedated state of mind.

Spirit One: Philip walks away.
Spirit Two: There's the zombie!

^: There's the Zombie

Next, two spirits talk about a drunk and a crook.

Spirit One: There goes the drunk.

Paranormal Investigations: The Cajun Ghost Hunter Chronicles

Spirit Two: He's a crook. I want to find him!

^: The Drunk

Then I heard a spirit that stated something that was very disturbing and graphic. What's fascinating about this EVP is that a singular voice lasts 2.87 seconds, which means that at a fifty-millisecond sweep rate, the spirit talked over fifty-seven radio frequencies!

Spirit: Rudolph's daddy shot off his head!

^: Shot Off His Head

Later that day, Philip and I went to the office. When we pulled up in the truck, some visitors were taking pictures, so we went up on the porch and discovered a milk crate that had some traps in it. They were too small to be bear traps, so I told Philip that they must be coon traps and would be good trigger objects to contact spirits. Philip then performed an EVP session asking the spirits if they used them to hunt. The intelligent response was immediate and most relevant to the question!

Philip: Y'all use those coon traps to hunt?
Spirit: Got coon trap!

^: Got Coon Trap

I went back to the quarters and performed an EVP session. I asked the spirits if they had killed any of the soldiers that came down there during the labor uprising in 1887. The spirit's response sounded like it belonged to a slave and had a malicious tone about it.

Stan: Did y'all kill any of those white men that came down here from the state militia?
Spirit: We fed your stink pit.

^: We Fed Your Stink Pit

Paranormal Investigations: The Cajun Ghost Hunter Chronicles

For those readers not familiar with graves in South Louisiana, most gravesites south of Baton Rouge are built above ground due to the proximity of the water table. Many tombs are family plots with four slots for bodies. As the relatives for these family plots die, the bones in the caskets in the slots are emptied into a pit below the tomb, creating spaces for the new bodies, and the old caskets are destroyed. The names of the newly deceased are added to the marble cover of the tomb where all the names of the family members are engraved. Hence, this gives meaning to the spirit's response of "We fed your stink pit"!

In this same session, there are six EVPs that are somehow related. Perhaps it was residual from a time during one of the yellow fever epidemics that occurred frequently in the mid-to-late 1800s and the early twentieth century in South Louisiana due to the mosquito infestations common around here. My own grandmother had yellow fever, and her father died in the bed next to her. Because of the contagion, his body had to be buried nearby in a graveyard for black people in Little Bayou Black, and the family had to wait a year and a day before they could move the body to the family plot at Saint Joseph's Cemetery in Thibodaux.

Spirit One: Smelling Death!
Spirit Two: I told her put a mask on!
Spirit Three: Death is busy around here!
Spirit Four: He's coming back here!
Spirit Five: Please, Jeff, help!
Spirit Six: It's priests they talked about, Stan!

$\triangle$: Smelling Death

We went back on June 18, 2011, and I was on the porch of the office, sitting on the bench.

Stan: Do y'all like me sitting on your porch?
Spirit: Keep off!

Paranormal Investigations: The Cajun Ghost Hunter Chronicles

⌃: Keep Off

A year later, as I was performing an EVP on the porch, a man drove up in a car and looked none too happy that I was there. I waved to him and headed down to the quarters and started an EVP session. A little while later, he drove up and asked if he could help me. I told him that I was just looking around. He told me to be sure to stay on this side of the barbed wire and to stay off the grounds around the office as that was private property. I told him I would and that I was just performing paranormal investigations around there. He replied that they don't like that sort of stuff around there! I told him to have a good day, and he drove off and turned down the lane to the main house.

I next picked up one spirit that said "Wasp nest" and another that said the juju was there. Evidently, a wasp nest was viewed as an item for magical uses, such as spells. It amazes me that in a slave quarters, I picked up voices that mention juju. The term *juju* and the practices associated with it travelled to the Americas from West Africa with the influx of slaves and still survive in some areas, particularly among the various groups of Maroons who have tended to preserve their African traditions. Today it refers specifically to objects, such as amulets, and spells used superstitiously as part of witchcraft in West Africa.

Spirit One: Wasp nest!
Spirit Two: The juju's here!

⌃: The Juju's Here

Contrary to common belief, voodoo (known as *vodun* in West Africa) is not related to juju despite the linguistic and spiritual similarities. Juju has acquired some karmic attributes in more recent times. Good juju can stem from almost any good deed: saving a kitten or returning a lost book. Bad juju can be spread just as easily. These ideas revolve around the luck and fortune portions of juju. The use of juju to describe an object usually involves small items worn or carried; these generally contain medicines produced by witch doctors.

Paranormal Investigations: The Cajun Ghost Hunter Chronicles

A week later, on June 25, 2011, Philip performed an EVP in front of the church in the quarters. He asked the spirits if they were all Christians, and a spirit said to someone to tell him that was right and that God will lift him up. Again, an EVP mentioning God.

Philip: Were y'all Christians . . . all of y'all?
Spirit One: Tell him that would be right!
Spirit Two: God will lift you up!

‿: God Will Lift You Up

I went back to the quarters on July 2, 2011, and went to the office to use the coon traps as trigger objects since we had such great success with them in the past few weeks. The EVP session that I performed while holding one paid off.

Stan: I got me a coon trap. What did y'all do with this?
Spirit: Bust it open.

‿: Bust It Open

Even though spirits don't eat, it is something that everyone enjoyed while they were in this life. Whenever I ask questions about food, I sometimes get some intelligent, relevant responses. Evidently, this spirit had his preference for turkey instead.

Stan: Oooh! Make me some coons with some sweet potatoes, yeah!
Spirit: Apples and blackened turkey!

‿: Apples and Blackened Turkey

Later in this session, a spirit spoke on Death. He actually told me I speak on Death. The spirits by now were getting used to me coming out there and knew what I was doing. In the words of Carlos Castaneda, Death is always looking over your left shoulder.

91

Paranormal Investigations: The Cajun Ghost Hunter Chronicles

Spirit One: Death walks here!
Spirit Two: Stanley, you speak on Death!

⌃: Death Walks Here

I went to the quarters on July 23. 2011, and performed an EVP in front of the church. I captured a few good EVPs during the session, but this one was the most profound.

Stan: God bless this church.
Spirit: God's life struck me!

⌃: God's Life Struck Me

I play this for my family and friends, and they wonder what this spirit means by that statement. I truly believe this spirit is describing the same ecstasy that St. Teresa of Avila writes about in her autobiography. She said, "It is impossible to describe or explain the way in which God wounds the soul, or the very pain that he inflicts on it, so that it hardly knows what it is doing. But this is so sweet a pain that no delight in the whole world can be more pleasing. The soul, as I have said, would be glad always to be dying of this ill." She went on to describe a vision she had where her heart was struck and pierced by the spear of a cherubim and said, "The sweetness caused by this intense pain is so extreme that one cannot possibly wish it to cease, nor is one's soul then content with anything but God."

Many women have had an epiphany or rapture of this sort and have gone on to enter convents and become nuns. When she read this biography overnight at a Catholic friend's house, St. Teresa Benedicta of the Cross (Edith Stein), who died in the crematory of Auschwitz, converted from Judaism to Catholicism and eventually became a Carmelite nun. Of course, I leave the interpretation and meaning of this EVP to the reader.

Paranormal Investigations: The Cajun Ghost Hunter Chronicles

In this session in front of the church, I also retrieved these EVPs about a Reverend Colston, and when I asked if he was there, another spirit asked me what I was looking for.

Spirit One: Stop it!
Spirit Two: Reverend Colston.
Spirit Three: Stanley!
Stan: Reverend, are you still here?
Spirit: Stanley, what you look for over here?

^: Reverend Colston

I went back to the quarters on August 13, 2011, and performed a session. I picked up some spirits that sounded like they were talking about Ruffin doing something bad to a girl and someone picking him up.

Spirit One: Ruffin, get off her!
Spirit Two: Big Ben . . . scared!
Spirit Three: My baby . . . pick up!
Spirit Four: They got Ruffin!

^: They Got Ruffin

In this same file, I asked the spirits to show themselves to the light in my camera, and they had a photographic reply.

Stan: Show yourself to the light in my camera!
Spirit: They did movie here!

^: They Did Movie Here

Actually, Hollywood movie directors (like the artists who have fallen under its spell) have been taken with the place. It was featured in the 1999 HBO movie *A Lesson Before Dying,* with Don Cheadle, and in the 1994 movie *Interview with a Vampire*, starring Tom Cruise, Brad Pitt, and Antonio Banderas.

Paranormal Investigations: The Cajun Ghost Hunter Chronicles

Two weeks later on August 27, 2011, I captured several ambient (no white noise) EVPs. The first is a man speaking of his sister. I find these types fascinating because if I had good hearing, I might hear disembodied voices like these at that time around me without having to wait and process the audio file when I get home. The background sound is cicadas singing their evening songs. It seems like the spirits use the insects' audio energy to express themselves!

Spirit: That's my sister!

‿: That's My Sister

The second ambient capture is a residual statement from a woman who talks about how they cleaned.

Spirit: They have never cleaned like that!

‿: They Have Never Cleaned Like That

I then asked the spirits in front of the church what they meant by the astounding statement, "God's life struck me." A spirit responds so gracefully. Trust me!

Stan: What did you mean, "God's life struck me?" How did his life strike you?
Spirit: Trust me!

‿: Trust Me

Being half-Polish and Catholic, I have to expound on the revelation of this response to me. On the twenty-second of February 1931, St. Faustina (Helen Kowalska) received the first revelation of the mercy of God. She wrote about it in her diary: "When I was in my cell at night, I saw the Lord Jesus dressed in white. One of his hands was lifted as if to give His blessing, and with the other hand, he touched his veil, which was slightly opened at the chest. Two long rays shone: one was

Paranormal Investigations: The Cajun Ghost Hunter Chronicles

red and the other was white. I remained in silence contemplating the Lord. My soul was fearful but also full of immense joy. After a while the Lord told me, 'Paint an image according to the pattern you see, with the signature: Jesus, I trust in You.'" Hence, the relevance of the statement "Trust me" comes to light.

In another three-minute, ambient EVP session on this day, I captured another eerie EVP when I asked the spirits about the statements made on May 27, 2011, about not liking people and killing them.

Stan: You don't like them. Kill them. Who don't you like, and why don't you like them?
Spirit: Clayton was killed!

⌃: Clayton Was Killed

Next, my son Philip performed an EVP session in front of a house that looked pretty dilapidated. When he asked about why this house was in such bad shape compared to the others, one spirit wanted to surprise him, and another disembodied voice sounded surprised himself that our communication with them was happening!

Philip: All the other houses are in pretty good condition. What happened to this one?
Spirit One: Let's surprise him!
Spirit Two: This is happening?!

⌃: This Is Happening

Philip then asked them about the mosquitoes and if any of them died from yellow fever. A spirit then responded in an insulting manner.

Philip: Did y'all hate the mosquitoes out here? Did they . . . did some of them kill you with yellow fever?
Spirit: You are nothing!

Paranormal Investigations: The Cajun Ghost Hunter Chronicles

⌃: You Are Nothing

I told Philip it was time to go, and as he said bye, we picked up this spirit talking about the temperature.

Stan: Come on. Let's go!
Philip: OK . . . bye!
Spirit: It's warm in here again.

⌃: It's Warm in Here

In this session, we had picked up two disembodied voices. The first one sounded like an older man pointing out his shed.

Spirit: That's my shed.

⌃: My Shed

The second voice was a residual talking about a cat.

Spirit: Oh, Leslie's cat!

⌃: Leslie's Cat

This was a very active day spiritually, and we not only captured all of these wonderful ambient EVPs on my RT-EVP recorder, but Philip also captured this disembodied voice on my infrared video camera while walking back to my car!

Spirit: John Himel, do you wanna play? Do something . . . with me?

⌃: John Himel

On September 18, 2011, I went to the quarters and captured this direct, intelligent response on a question of baked coon, which my Cajun grandmother used to fix and I miss eating.

96

Paranormal Investigations: The Cajun Ghost Hunter Chronicles

Stan: Boy, wouldn't some baked coon with some sweet potatoes be good right now?
Spirit: That would be . . . Heat it up!

^: Baked Coon

I then asked the spirits if any of them had died from the typhoid fever. Typhoid fever epidemics had swept the parishes in 1852, 1853, 1854, 1858, and 1861. The response was positive.

Stan: Did any of you die from typhoid fever?
Sprit One: Most did!
Spirit Two: We would please Death!

^: Most Did

On September 18, 2011, my wife, Barbara, out of the blue, asked me to get my equipment because she wanted to go out to Laurel Valley for me to perform a field investigation with her and her brother Harold, who was living with us and, like my son Philip, also suffered from PTSD from the war in Vietnam over forty years ago. I immediately grabbed my stuff because it's very rare that she actually wants to participate in my paranormal endeavors. We drove out there, and I set up my camera and performed an EVP session while she and Harold walked around the quarters. I acquired two very good EVPs. In the first one, I tried to provoke Edgar Fleeker, the individual that I am told by spirits committed a murder in the quarters, and I will detail my accounts later. Since I had EVPs telling me that he stabbed someone named Molly Dunn, I asked him what he would do to Barbara. The reply astonished me not only because of its richness of tone and clarity but also because of what he talked about.

Stan: Look, I brought Barbara. What would you do to her?
Spirit: Bring it by, Froo Froo!

^: Bring It by, Froo Froo

Paranormal Investigations: The Cajun Ghost Hunter Chronicles

The reason this is so surprising is because Froo Froo is my pet poodle, and this spirit wanted me to bring him by there! I will bring him by one day to see what sort of activity his presence will produce.

In the same session, I directed the spirits' attention to Barbara's brother, Harold, and asked them what his name was. The response was clear and correct!

Stan: What's that other man's name over there that's with me?
Spirit: Harold!

^: Harold

I performed one other EVP session that day and picked up this eerie one that was reverse speech. A spirit said that Philip shot his mammy, and another spirit, who may have been the mammy, said that he did.

Spirit One: Philip shot his mammy!
Spirit Two: Philip shot me!

^: Philip Shot His Mammy

On October 7, 2011, I stopped by the quarters to perform a short session on my way to do my weekly grocery shopping. Harold had recently moved in with us, until he could get on his feet. I captured this EVP from a spirit wanting me to promise him something important.

Spirit: Promise me . . . Harold staying!

^: Harold Staying

As I stated before, Harold is a Vietnam vet with 100 percent disability due to PTSD. He was in the 101st Airborne and was a tunnel rat. I had a feeling this was his dad and he wanted me to promise him that I would allow Harold to stay with us until he was ready to go out on

Paranormal Investigations: The Cajun Ghost Hunter Chronicles

his own. I love Harold like my own brother and will always give him refuge for life!

On October 15, 2011, I returned to the slave quarters and performed a three-minute session. There were a couple of spirits that talked about someone named W beating on Chad in Houma, which is twenty miles away, and someone named Edward Coffey hitting on him. The clarity and reference to the nearby town made posting this one worth it.

Spirit One: W beat Chad in Houma!
Spirit Two: Edward Coffey hit on him!

⌃: W Beat Chad

Of course, I had to use the idea of eating some food to generate a spirit response during this session. It definitely yielded an intelligent, direct response to my question about chitlins, a popular food amongst black folks.

Stan: How about some chitlins for supper?
Spirit: A pork chitlins will be good!

⌃: Chitlins

I then picked up this spirit voice pointing out Cathy's beau. What is fascinating about these two statements in this EVP by the same spirit is that they are the reverse speech of each other. Only spirits can produce intelligent speech in the reverse waveform that is produced during processing. In chemistry, two chemical structures that are mirror images of each other are called enantiomers. Rotation of the compounds in three dimensions will not allow the structures to be superimposed, yet the two distinct, separate compounds can exist in nature with the same number of elements. In reverse speech from the spirit realm, the waveforms are mirror images of each other, but instead of intelligent forward speech and reverse gibberish, the reverse

Paranormal Investigations: The Cajun Ghost Hunter Chronicles

speech is sometimes an intelligent statement. And in many cases, such as this one, the meaning is related to the forward speech!

Spirit Forward Speech: There's Ms. Cathy's beau right there.
Spirit Reverse Speech: Take your beau to Cathy's grandma.

^: Cathy's Beau

On November 25, 2011, I went to the quarters and performed an EVP session. When I asked the spirits to talk to my blinking red light, they gave a positive response.

Stan: Come talk into my blinking red light.
Spirit: Red!

^: Red

On December 2, 2011, I returned to Laurel Valley, and in the EVP session, I obtained some very clear class-A EVPs, a few that were disturbing. In the first one, a spirit said that she likes this man named Malcolm.

Spirit: I think I like Malcolm.

^: Malcolm

Here are the EVPs that I found disturbing. I put them all together because I feel that they are related around an incident where someone's sister was killed or wounded.

Spirit One: Philip, your baby's not in bed!
Spirit Two: What's wrong?
Spirit Three: He killed my sister!
Spirit Four: Whatever is happening . . . he shot her!

Paranormal Investigations: The Cajun Ghost Hunter Chronicles

Maybe she was discovered not to be home after she went out because her boyfriend had killed her. I can only speculate, so I leave these residual EVPs of this tragedy to the reader's imagination. Being a community with a large slave population for thirty-plus years, this was one of probably several tragic incidents that left a residual imprint of negative spiritual energy.

^: He Shot Her

Two weeks later on December 17, 2011, I went to the quarters and picked up this EVP about someone named Frank.

Spirit One: Frank's dead!
Spirit Two: Frank is dead!

^: Frank's Dead

On December 29, 2011, I went to Laurel Valley and performed an EVP where a spirit knew my name. It's exciting when they say my first name, but I was thrilled when I heard him say both my first and middle name!

Stan: What is my name?
Spirit: Stanley Paul!

^: Stanley Paul

On March 17, 2012, I went to the quarters and enticed the spirits with pork chitlins again. I received two different responses to the same question. The first direct, intelligent response follows.

Stan: Boy, wouldn't some pork chitlins be good right now?
Spirit: That's awesome!

^: That's Awesome

101

Paranormal Investigations: The Cajun Ghost Hunter Chronicles

Here's the second response. It's residual but related to the question concerning food.

Stan: Boy, wouldn't some pork chitlins be good right now?
Spirit: Your daddy left food!

‸: Your Daddy Left Food

In the same session, I had three EVPs that I put together since they seem related. The first spirit talked about Vernon killing someone, the second said to get Michelle because they were hard on him and there was blood, and the third was a lamentation about missing Germaine.

Spirit One: Vernon said kill ya . . . now I'm dead!
Spirit Two: Get Michelle! They were hard on him . . . blood!
Spirit Three: Germaine . . . we miss him! Oh god, we miss him!

‸: Oh God, We Miss Him

I then went in front of the church and performed a session with my video camera pointed at the church in front of my Auxio speakers that were connected to my RT-EVP recorder scanning FM frequencies at fifty milliseconds per station. I had an intelligent conversation with the spirits and pieced all the questions and answers together, eliminating the dead time in between responses.

Stan: What is your name?
Spirit: George.
Stan: George? Hi, George, I'm Stan.
Spirit: Hi, Stan.
Stan: Hey, George! How'd you die?
Spirit: Choked!
Stan: Can I get a "Praise the Lord" or a "Hallelujah"?
Spirit: Pray to God!
Stan: Edgar Fleeker, are you here?
Spirit: Dead!

Paranormal Investigations: The Cajun Ghost Hunter Chronicles

Stan: You're dead?
Spirit: Shot!

^: Shot

On March 24, 2012, I performed an EVP session in front of the church in the quarters, and I obtained some relevant responses when I asked the spirits if they saw Jesus Christ! What a joy to capture so many positive responses to my question in one three-minute session. I put them all together since they are all related to this religious site of spiritual activity.

Stan: Praise the Lord, do y'all see Jesus Christ?
Spirit One: I think so!
Spirit Two: I got saved!
Spirit Three: Praise God!
Spirit Four: My prayer is my hope!

^: My Prayer Is My Hope

On March 31, 2012, I stopped by Laurel Valley to perform an EVP session and asked the spirits what was my name. This had to be a spirit that was a close family member because they were the only ones who called me Stanley Junior since I was named after my father.

Stan: What is my name?
Spirit: Stanley Junior.

^: Stanley Junior

On April 14, 2012, at the quarters, I received this EVP pronouncing that most people get out of there. Perhaps they were referring to the freemen after the Civil War who wanted a better life since they were no longer slaves and could move to other places to pursue their dreams instead of being sharecroppers for the rest of their lives.

103

Paranormal Investigations: The Cajun Ghost Hunter Chronicles

Spirit: Most people get out of here!

⌃: Most People Get Out

On May 5, 2012, I captured these two EVPs while conducting a session in the slave quarters. I put them together since the slaves came forward and they know how much I love going to the plantation to visit them and conduct my investigations. What fascinated me after I made this is that the spirit voices singsong like a chorus, and though the statements they make are at separate times in the recording, the voices sound the same—like they are from the same chorus!

Stan: Are there any slaves walking around here today?
Spirit One: Slaves are here for that!
Spirits Two: He loves the people here!

⌃: Slaves Are Here for That

Before I go to the next part of this Laurel Valley Plantation treatise, I will leave the reader with this EVP captured on March 24, 2012, where I asked the original owner, Etienne Boudreaux, if he was walking his fields. I received a positive response from a very old spirit, so the vocalization is somewhat robotic in nature.

Stan: Etienne Boudreaux, are you walking your fields?
Spirit: I walk field!

⌃: I Walk Field

IX

LAUREL VALLEY PLANTATION AND EDGAR FLEEKER

http://cajunghosthunter.com/EVPs_Laurel_Valley_I.php

http://cajunghosthunter.com/EVPs__Edgar_Fleeker__II.html

I had received some very faint EVPs on May 27, 2011, that told of a man named Edgar Fleeker who killed a girl named Molly Dunn. After hearing these EVPs, I pursued questioning the spirits every time I went out there to find out if there is a story that connects these EVPs. The one that initially talks about him is too faint to post as a video/EVP on the website. I will start my presentation of EVPs from the sessions that I collected on the next day, May 28, 2011. All the EVPs posted in this chapter are related to this story, and as time goes on, you will see how the responses to my questions fill in the pieces of the puzzle for this possible murder with some intelligent, direct responses to my questions.

In the first EVP that I captured, there was a ghost whisperer that told me the girl's name.

Spirit: And the girl's name was Molly Dunn.

$\triangle$: Molly Dunn

I then picked up this very disturbing EVP from a spirit that said what Edgar did to her. Could this possibly have been Molly Dunn?

Spirit: Edgar did horrible, horrible things to me!

$\triangle$: Horrible

Paranormal Investigations: The Cajun Ghost Hunter Chronicles

There was a spirit that then talked about the heritage of Edgar.

Spirit: Edgar's a Dubois . . . Shoot him!

^: Edgar's a Dubois

Another spirit asked if Edgar had been shot dead.

Spirit: Have you shot Edgar dead?

^: Shot Edgar Dead

In the last EVP that I captured on this day, I asked the spirits how many times he'd stabbed Molly Dunn.

Stan: I heard Edgar Fleeker stabbed her. How many times did he stab her?
Spirit: Forty!

^: Forty

In another session on the same day, I captured this eerie EVP. It's like a spirit walked in on something he wasn't expecting, and another spirit asked him to commit murder.

Spirit One: He set us up!
Spirit Two: Won't you stab her with me?

^: Stab Her with Me

On June 4, 2011, I returned to the slave quarters. I performed one session with an FM scan and captured some intelligent responses to my questions regarding Edgar Fleeker. I asked the spirits if they hung him for killing Molly Dunn. The spirit didn't know him and answered my question with a question.

Paranormal Investigations: The Cajun Ghost Hunter Chronicles

Stan: Did they hang Edgar Fleeker for killing Molly Dunn?
Spirit: Who is Edgar Fleeker?

^: Who Is Edgar Fleeker?

I processed the reverse speech of the spirit's response to this question, and instead of asking who he is, the spirit acknowledged that Edgar is her baby. I wonder, was this Edgar Fleeker's mother speaking?

Stan: Did they hang Edgar Fleeker for killing Molly Dunn?
Spirit: My kid is Edgar Fleeker!

^: My Kid Is Edgar Fleeker

They then told me that Edgar killed someone named Ju Be.

Spirit: Edgar killed Ju Be!

^: Edgar Killed Ju Be

Another spirit then said that Edgar had killed his dad. The reverse speech said Edgar Fleeker's name! I pasted the forward and reverse speech together because of their relevance to each other.

Spirit: Edgar Fleeker, he killed my dad!

^: Killed My Dad

Then, a spirit mentioned that someone was Edgar Fleeker's cousin. What fascinates me is that spirits are continuously saying his whole name!

Spirit: He's Edgar Fleeker's cousin.

^: Edgar's Cousin

Paranormal Investigations: The Cajun Ghost Hunter Chronicles

A spirit then asked someone, I'm assuming it's Edgar, to explain why he kills.

Spirit: Tell her why you kill!

⌒: Why You Kill

The following week on June 11, 2011, I went back and resumed my questioning. I asked the spirits if Edgar Fleeker killed them.

Stan: Did Edgar Fleeker kill you?
Spirit: Now they're dead!

⌒: Now They're Dead

I next asked the question that a spirit finally answered directly by asserting that Edgar killed Molly Dunn.

Stan: Who did Edgar Fleeker stab forty times?
Spirit: Edgar Fleeker killed Molly Dunn!

⌒: Killed Molly Dunn

On June 25, 2012, when I returned to the quarters, I asked this spirit named Kathy Mouton if Edgar had done terrible things to her.

Stan: Kathy Mouton, did Edgar Fleeker do terrible, terrible things to you?
Spirit: And also hurt me badly.

⌒: Hurt Me Badly

When I visited on July 25, 2012, I asked Kathy once again what he did to her.

Stan: Kathy Mouton, what did Edgar Fleeker do to you?

Paranormal Investigations: The Cajun Ghost Hunter Chronicles

Spirit: He shoot me!

^: He Shoot Me

In an August 13, 2012, EVP, a spirit told me that he didn't kill her. Was she referring to Edgar Fleeker?

Spirit: He didn't kill me!

^: He Didn't Kill Me

Two weeks later, I asked Edgar Fleeker if his spirit was there, and a spirit told me he knew him.

Stan: Edgar Fleeker, is your spirit roaming here?
Spirit: I know Edgar Fleeker.

^: I Know Edgar Fleeker

I then tried to get spirits excited by saying Edgar Fleeker was coming. Instead of voicing their fears, they told me that my wife was scared of him. At the time, Barbara was insecure from my investigations about Edgar Fleeker and feared that I would bring his spirit home with me.

Stan: Run! Here comes Edgar Fleeker!
Spirit: Barbara scared of him!

^: Barbara Scared

On September 14, 2012, I was standing in front of the houses in the slave quarters and asked the whereabouts of Edgar.

Stan: Where is Edgar Fleeker?
Spirit: He don't live in here!

^: Don't Live in Here

Paranormal Investigations: The Cajun Ghost Hunter Chronicles

When I visited on September 18, 2012, I asked Edgar if he was there. He replied in a chilling manner!

Stan: Edgar Fleeker, are you here?
Spirit: I killed them!

⌢: I Killed Them

My weekly visits subsided, and it was a month later on October 15, 2012, when I stopped by. I asked the spirits where he was, and a spirit mentioned his first name.

Stan: Where is Edgar Fleeker?
Spirit: Hey, I leave with Edgar this morning!

⌢: I Leave This Morning

Another month passed, and on November 25, 2012, I paid a visit. I asked if Edgar was there and received an affirmative answer from him. The manner that he responded was strange because he called me Doc. This reminded me of my grandfather Assie Jolet when he would greet my dad as he walked into his house. My dad was a med tech, and my pawpaw would ask him, "What's up, Doc?"

Stan: Edgar Fleeker, are you here?
Spirit: Hey, Doc! I'm here!

⌢: Hey, Doc

A week later on December 2, 2011, I asked Edgar if he was there. I received a very low-voiced, eerie response.

Stan: Are you here?
Spirit: Yes!

⌢: Yes

Paranormal Investigations: The Cajun Ghost Hunter Chronicles

I returned on December 17, 2011, and performed an ambient EVP. I asked Molly Dunn what Edgar did to her. I received a disparaging voice from a spirit that seemed to have suffered!

Stan: Molly Dunn, what did Edgar Fleeker do to you?
Spirit: He hurt me!

^: He Hurt Me

I didn't get any more intelligent responses to my questions about Edgar Fleeker until March 17, 2012. When I asked if he was present, a spirit replied that he was her father!

Stan: Edgar Fleeker, are you here?
Spirit: My father was Edgar Fleeker!

^: My Father

The following week, I asked Molly Dunn about her stabbing.

Stan: Molly Dunn, how many times did Edgar Fleeker stab you?
Spirit: Seven! So now I'm dead!

^: Now I'm Dead

When I returned on March 31, 2012, I asked Edgar Fleeker how many times he got shot. He replied that they shot him!

Stan: Edgar Fleeker, I heard you were shot! How many times did you get shot?
Spirit: They shot me!

^: They Shot Me

Paranormal Investigations: The Cajun Ghost Hunter Chronicles

In this same EVP session, I captured a spirit's voice saying that he loved to cut up the bishop. Were they referring to Edgar and his obsession with stabbing people?

Spirit: He cut the bishop! He loved to cut him up!

^: Cut the Bishop

Two weeks later on April 13, 2012, I asked Edgar if he had been shot.

Stan: Where did they shoot you?
Spirit: Took one hit!

^: Took One Hit

I then asked him why he got shot. His response indicated that he was at the bottom of the social class and that he couldn't avoid the consequences of his actions.

Stan: Why did they shoot you?
Spirit: 'Cause no po' man can duck prison!

^: No Po' Man Can Duck Prison

Three weeks later on May 5, 2012, I received this spirit imploring Edgar to go home.

Spirit: Edgar, go home!

^: Edgar, Go Home

In this same session, I asked Molly Dunn what Edgar did to her.

Stan: Molly Dunn, what did Edgar Fleeker do to you?
Spirit: He attacked me!

114

Paranormal Investigations: The Cajun Ghost Hunter Chronicles

‸: He Attacked Me

I then performed an ambient EVP, and when I asked Edgar if he was there, I captured a spirit saying that he just wants to kill now!

Stan: Edgar Fleeker, are you here?
Spirit: He just wants to kill now someone!

‸: He Just Wants to Kill

That concludes my treatise on Edgar Fleeker. I have looked for Edgar Fleeker in the history of Laurel Valley Plantation online, but I can't find a record of his name. I will get with the Friends of Laurel Valley to see if they can give me any information on lists that may exist of the freemen or the sharecroppers that occupied Laurel Valley. I will continue to visit the quarters as it is peaceful, and I'm sure the spirits will continue to talk to me and tell me about their troubles with Edgar Fleeker. I will have to continue to ask the same question as the spirit on June 4, 2011: "Who is Edgar Fleeker?"

X

LAS VEGAS AND VICINITY

http://cajunghosthunter.com/Las_Vegas_I.html

http://cajunghosthunter.com/Las_Vegas_II.html

http://cajunghosthunter.com/Las_Vegas_III.html

We took a trip at the end of July 2011 to stay at a resort in Las Vegas as part of a promotion from a time-share I had purchased. We had planned our Las Vegas vacation months before I had purchased my EVP recorder, but after I obtained it, I created an itinerary on where I would use it. On one of the numerous paranormal programs on television, I had seen an episode where the investigators visited the Bonnie Springs Ranch in Blue Diamond, Nevada.

Originally built in 1843, it was a stopping place for the wagon trains going to California on the Old Spanish Trail. General Fremont stopped here in 1846 on his way to California to gear up for the trip through Death Valley. It has been used as a tourist attraction since 1952. It is often called an oasis in the desert where one can stop for a cool drink of springwater. On the grounds is an excellent, quaint restaurant serving home-style food. There is also a motel with fireplaces, Jacuzzis, and a stable with many horses to ride on the surrounding trails. There is even a small zoo with native and nonnative animals.

Many buildings are featured on the property. There is an old-style saloon that offers small drinks and snacks; an opera house where small-time performances are held; a small schoolhouse with a playground in front of it that has a merry-go-round for the children; a wax museum that shows sculptures of the Paiute Indians and other types of people, such as priests and explorers; and many other smaller buildings.

119

Paranormal Investigations: The Cajun Ghost Hunter Chronicles

We drove up Highway 159 toward Red Rock Canyon on July 30, 2011, and took a left on Bonnie Springs Ranch Road. It was our first time among the giant cacti plants, and we stopped on the side of the road to take pictures. As we walked on the first trail to the right of the road, among the brush was a memorial rock with an inscription that read, "Nick . . . may your spirit soar." I proceeded to perform an EVP session with my RT-EVP recorder with an FM scan at fifty milliseconds.

I asked Nick how old he was when he died. A spirit replied in the same voice throughout the 3.5-second response that he lost his thumb and asked if I had clapped for Nick.

Stan: How old were you when you died?
Spirit: He lost his thumb. Did y'all clap for Nick?

⌃: Did Y'all Clap for Nick?

Other spirits responded that they couldn't hear the heartbeat. As I wrote about this, I took the response and reversed the speech to listen for more information. I couldn't understand the first two words, but the last four saying that he was sick and had a heart attack were very relevant to the forward response. I placed the reverse response after the forward response for the EVP file posted on the website. After I heard the reverse speech response, I had to delete what I had originally wrote stating that I still wondered how he died after listening to the forward speech. The reverse speech answered that question for me sixteen months later!

Stan: How old were you when you died?
Sprits: Listen, there's no heartbeat! Heart attack . . . he's sick!

⌃: There's No Heartbeat

I asked if there were any cowboys or miners roaming the hills. A spirit replied that he is a soldier.

Paranormal Investigations: The Cajun Ghost Hunter Chronicles

Stan: Are there any cowboys or miners roaming these hills?
Spirit: I'm a soldier!

△: I'm a Soldier

I then wanted to know if there were any spirits of Indians present since the Paiute Indians had inhabited those hills in the past.

Stan: Are there any Indians roaming these hills?
Spirit: I am Celsa!

△: I Am Celsa

This name is fascinating because *celsa* is Latin for "very spiritual." So a spirit told me they were very spiritual!

We then proceeded to the town of Bonnie Springs after waiting on the road for a herd of mules and burros to walk by. One of the mules just kind of stood there for a while, and a lady coming from the opposite direction on her way out had to get out of her SUV to coax it and the others to the side of the road.

Once we arrived at the ticket booth, I realized that the person running the booth had actually been on one of the paranormal TV shows that I watch! I asked him if it was OK to take EVP recordings, and he said yes; we just had to make sure that we didn't bother the other visitors.

We went inside of the gates and started walking through the buildings down the Main Street. We stopped in the gift shop and looked around. I performed an EVP in the far corner of the shop. I figured that if I talked like a cowboy that a spirit would respond in like fashion. They did not disappoint me!

Stan: Howdy, pardner!
Spirit: Howdy! Howdy! Oh yeah!

121

Paranormal Investigations: The Cajun Ghost Hunter Chronicles

⌢: Howdy

We continued down the Main Street and then took the right that brought us to the merry-go-round in front of the schoolhouse. Witnesses have reported this merry-go-round turning on its own on windless days. I turned on my EVP recorder and captured a couple of voices making statements related to children playing on a playground.

Spirit: Isaac could get the ball.

⌢: Get the Ball

Spirit: I pick up rocks and throw them bigger than that!

⌢: I Pick Up Rocks

There were some children on a tour a little ways up the street, so I asked the spirits if they would like to play with them. The spirit's response was amorous toward me!

Stan: You hear the voices of the children? Wouldn't you like to play with them? Wouldn't you like that?
Spirit: I love you!

⌢: I Love You

We then walked up to the schoolhouse. Visitors were not allowed inside, but the door was open with a rope across the entrance, so I proceeded with an EVP session to determine why the spirit of a young girl had been seen haunting the premises. I asked her why she haunted the schoolhouse. The response mentioned a gruff man that took her in a bedroom, and another response mentioned a poor little girl. Was there a possible rape that occurred on the premises and that's the reason for the spirit's haunting?

122

Paranormal Investigations: The Cajun Ghost Hunter Chronicles

Stan: Why do you haunt this building? What happened to you that you're still in this schoolhouse?
Spirit One: Gruff man take me bedroom!
Spirit Two: Poor little girl!

^: Poor Little Girl

We went back up the street and stopped in front of the opera house. Unfortunately, it was closed to visitors, so I performed an EVP session on the front porch. I first picked up a clear voice that sounded like a cowhand, and he mentioned working in Bonnie Hills.

Spirit: I'm here serving a sprawl in Bonnie Hills!

^: Serving a Sprawl

I next asked if there was an evil spirit that roams around the premises since I had heard about this on one of the paranormal TV programs that I watch. The spirit told me that he's not dead, and the reverse speech said "Ben Godchaux," so I guess this meant that he was still wandering around.

Stan: Is there an evil spirit that lurks around here?
Spirit: He's not dead. Ben Godchaux!

^: Evil Spirit

I wanted to know why they ran to get out of there. A spirit responded that he was scared.

Stan: Why do you run to get outta here?
Spirit: I'm scared of him!

^: I'm Scared of Him

A spirit then said to come out to Vegas.

Paranormal Investigations: The Cajun Ghost Hunter Chronicles

Spirit: Come up to Vegas . . . got that?

‿: Come Up to Vegas

During one of the paranormal shows, they emphasized the fact that there is a spirit in the opera house that pushes and shoves people. I asked the spirit why he pushes and shoves people. A spirit replied that he's too weird, and in the reverse speech, he said that he resists and slaps people.

Stan: Why do you push and shove people?
Spirit: Because he's too weird. He resists and slaps people.

‿: Slaps People

We then walked over to the saloon. I did a quick EVP session when the only other customers in there walked out, but they started playing music halfway into the session. I did capture a residual spirit talking about Becky stabbing Sam for screwing around on her!

Stan: Is there a spirit in here?
Spirit: Sam f—cked around . . . Stab him, Becky!

‿: Stab Him, Becky

Although the wax museum and opera house were closed, we did capture some wonderful EVPs in all the other buildings around the premises. We will always remember our Western experience at the Bonnie Springs Ranch!

The next day, we went to the Rancho/Charleston area of the old Scotch 80's section of Las Vegas where the La Palazza mansion is located. The history of the mansion is tied to the mob during the days when the underworld controlled the casinos and clubs of Las Vegas. Recently since 2000, the former owner was once having a party, and an entity started sliding a wine glass down the rack, bringing it to the end where

Paranormal Investigations: The Cajun Ghost Hunter Chronicles

it fell onto the floor. When the owner got a sword down from its display in the room and started waving it to challenge the entity, a force started choking him! One of his friends had to grab him and haul him outside to get the entity to release the choke hold it had on him. After that, the owner started having violent outbursts of anger at a moment's notice, which was out of character for him, until he eventually had to move into another house that he owned just to maintain his sanity.

His girlfriend who lived with him also had some paranormal experiences in the house. While showering, she would hear disembodied voices making perverted statements, causing her to shorten the duration of her shower activities. They also discovered a secret room in the house that was behind two gold swan towel racks. It was constructed of all-white tile and had a drain in the middle of the room—a room perfect for killing someone and hosing the blood down the drain! The couple had pulled the sink out of the room and discovered caked blood behind it. A medium had once visited the house and sensed men on their knees with their hands behind their heads in a classic position for mob-style executions. She also had sensed women being assaulted and murdered in the room.

One of the paranormal shows that I watch once had a girl that looked like the former owner's girlfriend come in the house during their investigation, and they captured an EVP that said, "Kill her!"

Barbara and I arrived and parked about a block from the house. I proceeded to the front of the house in front of the locked gate to perform a six-minute EVP session. There were some neighbors outside across the street, but they went inside a little while after I had arrived. Barbara went walking down the street to admire the elegant homes in the subdivision.

In this EVP session, I captured some spirits that exemplify the history of this place and the evil assaults and murders that took place there. In my first EVP, I asked if there was an evil spirit. They told me they'd shoot me and to keep out!

125

Paranormal Investigations: The Cajun Ghost Hunter Chronicles

Stan: Is there evil in here?
Spirit One: They'll shoot ya!
Spirit Two: Keep out!

∧: Keep Out

I then asked if they had killed prostitutes in the house. A spirit replied that she had been shot and told Percy that Arthur had hurt her.

Stan: Did y'all kill prostitutes in the room of this house?
Spirit: He shot me in the bedroom! Arthur hurt me, Percy!

∧: He Shot Me

I captured this voice that asked someone named Dijon to bring Isabella home and another voice that said he'd just kill her.

Spirit One: Dijon, why can't you bring Isabella home?
Spirit Two: He'd just kill her!

∧: He'd Just Kill Her

Next, there were two voices that seemed to talk about hiding in the Palazza; perhaps they were referring to the secret, hidden murder room where the atrocities took place.

Spirit One: Hide your Palazza!
Spirit Two: Hidden. Get in back!

∧: Hide Your Palazza

There was this EVP with forward and reverse speech that claimed that Beth brings acid and that it's happening with her. I guess they meant she's got it going on because she supplies a drug for a party high. Another spirit named Clara immediately commented that she was into that!

Paranormal Investigations: The Cajun Ghost Hunter Chronicles

Spirit One: Beth brings your acid! It's happening with Beth!
Spirit Two: Clara's into that!

‸: Clara's into That

A voice then said that Dana didn't like this freak. The voice started high and then went into a decrescendo to end in a very low bass voice. Was she referring to me?

Spirit: Dana doesn't like this freak!

‸: Freak

Sometimes as a means of punishment for failing to pay a gambling debt or to get someone to talk, the mob would break peoples' fingers or legs. I captured this EVP that states such a fact.

Spirit: My finger's broken!

‸: Finger's Broken

During the EVP session, I heard these three different voices that talked about Thompson bleeding and that someone named Vincent Fonio shot him. I put all these voices together into one EVP since they seemed related and highlighted the murders that probably occurred there during the darker days of La Palazza.

Spirit One: Vincent Fonio shot him!
Spirit Two: Thompson bled! He shot him!
Spirit Three: Was he asleep or not?

‸: Thompson Bled

Because of the evil associated with La Palazza and the EVPs that I produced that talked about assaults and shootings, I'm glad that I was

Paranormal Investigations: The Cajun Ghost Hunter Chronicles

only able to conduct my investigation from the street in the middle of the afternoon.

The next day, Barbara and I went up to Mount Charleston for lunch at a restaurant/lodge near the peak. We planned to drive back to the east side of Old Las Vegas after lunch as I had planned an overnight stay at the Four Queens Hotel and Casino on Fremont Street. The hotel was opened in 1966 and named after the owner's, Ben Goffstein's, four daughters: Faith, Hope, Benita, and Michele. It has 690 rooms and a forty-thousand-square-foot casino.

We had a suite that was really inexpensive for one night. The casino comped us each $10 in free play, and I made $20 on top of that playing slots, so essentially, our stay was free.

I performed two EVP sessions in our room that evening. In the first session, I picked up a spirit who said that Dan Whittle was a bad cop.

Spirit: Dan Whittle was a bad cop.

‸: Bad Cop

I then asked if anyone had lost a lot of money and committed suicide. They said I was mean and why not kill them! They must think that I'd just as soon kill them rather than ask if they committed suicide!

Stan: Did anyone here lose a lot of money and commit suicide?
Spirit One: He's mean!
Spirit Two: Why not kill me, Stanley!

‸: Kill Me, Stanley

At the end of this session, I captured three voices saying in one sentence that they were a cop named Mick Janavilla. In the reverse speech, they said Howard's nothing and to lock him up. How relevant

Paranormal Investigations: The Cajun Ghost Hunter Chronicles

that he said he's a cop in forward speech and to lock someone up in the reverse speech!

Spirits: I'm a cop . . . Mick Janavilla. Howard nothing! Lock him up!

△: I'm a Cop

In my next session, I captured voices that, like in La Palazza, reflected the activities of the mafia in Las Vegas in the '60s and '70s. In the first EVP, I heard a voice tell Johnny that someone named Matt put a hit on them and tell in the reverse speech that they should be out of there, reminiscent of paying someone for a revenge killing.

Spirit: Hey, Johnny, Matt Kuslapak put a hit on you! We should be out of here!

△: Hey, Johnny

I then picked up a voice telling someone in forward speech that they will be there at five eight. In the reverse speech, they then said they'll help her kill Leon.

Spirit: I'll be arriving at five eight. Then we'll help her kill Leon!

△: Kill Leon

Finally, I captured this spirit who said that someone named Big Eddie was shot and he can't see them. Perhaps this spirit was hidden in the room when Big Eddie was shot and avoided getting killed himself. In the reverse speech, he stated that Big Eddie was dead and they just lost him!

Spirit: Big Eddie's shot! He can't see me! And he's dead! We just lost Big Eddie!

△: Big Eddie's Shot

129

Paranormal Investigations: The Cajun Ghost Hunter Chronicles

Two days later, Barbara and I went to the China Ranch Date Farm near the Amargosa Canyon and Tecopa, California, in Death Valley. The owner and friend of ours from the Samosa Factory in Las Vegas, Rick Aco, had recommended the farm to us during our visit to his wonderful establishment. I didn't capture many EVPs in the desert, but one that I captured resonates within me forever.

A Chinese man named either Quon Sing or Ah Foo came to this canyon after many years of work in the Death Valley borax mines according to available sources. He raised meat for the local mining camps and developed the water, planting fruits and vegetables. It became known as Chinaman's Ranch. A man named Morrison appeared sometime around 1900, and he ran the Chinese farmer off at gunpoint and claimed the ranch for his own. The name stuck even after Morrison eventually sold out. The farm then went through several owners and served as farm, cattle ranch, hog farm, alfalfa farm, and others.

Charles Brown Jr. and Bernice Sorrells, the son and daughter of area pioneer and longtime state senator Charles Brown of Shoshone, purchased the property in 1970. It remains in these families today.

In the early 1920s, Vonola Modine, youngest daughter of Death Valley area pioneer RJ Fairbanks, planted the date grove from seeds. Approximately half of the trees are male and produce only pollen. The females bear in the fall, each yielding from one hundred to three hundred pounds of dates in a season.

We drove up there early on a Tuesday morning, arriving around lunchtime. We proceeded to walk down one of the many trails. We didn't have hiking shoes, so we didn't plan to go too far down the trail. Barbara was having problems with sand flies chasing her, and she was constantly swatting them away as we walked down the trail. I started an EVP session, and I walked off the trail when I spotted some pieces of wood that looked like they may have been used to support a mine shaft. As I touched the wood, I asked if there were the spirits of old miners walking around there. The response was immediate, and it

Paranormal Investigations: The Cajun Ghost Hunter Chronicles

sounded like an angel giving me a profound message from the other side. She said that there was a spirit who loved me.

Stan: Are there any spirits of old miners wandering around here right now?
Spirit: There's a spirit who loves you!

⌃: A Spirit Loves You

We then returned back to the gift shop and had a wonderful milk shake made with dates. After purchasing a few items, we wandered around the grounds, looking at the trees, and on the way out stopped at the small building that housed their modest museum. I asked the original owner, Ah Foo, if he was present, and I captured another profound message telling me to get salvation.

Stan: Ah Foo . . . are you here?
Spirit: Get salvation!

⌃: Get Salvation

On our final day in the city of Las Vegas, we went to one last place, the Old Las Vegas Mormon Fort, recommended by Rick Aco of the Samosa Factory. On June 14 of 1855, William Bringhurst and his party of missionaries from the Church of Jesus Christ of Latter-day Saints arrived and settled along a creek in a meadow after traveling thirty-five days from Salt Lake City, Utah. Their mission was to establish a settlement between Utah and the Pacific coast in the Mexican territory. The settlement served the purpose of establishing peaceful relations with the Paiute Indians to convert them to Mormonism and to establish a station halfway between Utah and the settlements in California.

They built a fort, farmed the land from seeds and fruit trees brought from California, and were self-sustaining at the end of the first year. They built a school for the children and some of the Indians and established the post office where William Bringhurst was the first postmaster general of Las Vegas. In 1857, Brigham Young ran out of funds to support the distant settlements. Because of the difficulties the Mormons were having with the federal government and the land being too alkaline to sustain the food supply for the inhabitants, the fort had to be abandoned. Most of the missionaries returned to Utah.

Albert Knapp, the brother of William Knapp and who was a friend of Octavius Decatur Gass, returned to the fort in 1860 to set up a store to supply travelers and miners along the Old Spanish Trail. He returned to California in 1864 and died. His brother partnered with O. D. Gass to build a ranch and retain the store at the abandoned fort. Using part of the foundation and walls of the old fortification and the local Natives for labor, in 1865, OD set about building the ranch. He called it Los Vegas Rancho. He changed the spelling so as not to confuse the ranch with Las Vegas, New Mexico, another Mormon settlement about five hundred miles east. For nearly twenty years, the ranch had sufficient water and would support enough livestock, fruit trees, and vegetable crops to keep OD in business. Gass defaulted on a loan to Archibald Stewart in 1881 and lost the ranch, with Stewart and his wife, Helen, becoming the new caretakers.

Helen Stewart was a college-educated woman, and Archie had promised her that the move to the ranch would only be temporary. They moved there with their two sons in 1882 and established a thriving business selling wine and supplies to the local miners and travelers. Helen went on to have three more children while at the ranch before tragedy struck in 1884.

While William was away delivering produce and livestock to hungry miners in El Dorado Canyon, a ranch hand of his, Schyler Henry, decided to quit his job and approached Helen for his pay. Helen refused, telling him that he would have to wait for Archie's return since she didn't know how much he was owed. He proceeded to curse and threaten Helen, but she stood her ground, refusing to give him any wages. Henry left and went a couple of miles away to the Kiel ranch, which was operated by Conrad Kiel and his son, Edwin.

132

Paranormal Investigations: The Cajun Ghost Hunter Chronicles

Archie arrived home, and Helen told her husband about the provocative encounter she had with Henry. After a short rest and a meal, Archie saddled his horse back up despite pleas from Helen to let the incident go and stay home. He rode to the Kiel ranch, searching for Henry.

Hank Parrish and Jack Longstreet were two of the bad men, outlaws, and scoundrels that sought the Kiel ranch as a safe haven and hangout. Archie arrived and walked slowly to the back of the house after tying his horse behind a growth of grapevines. Archie was spotted after he discovered all the doors and windows of the house wide open. He fired the first shot and missed. After a short firefight ensued, Stewart was dead with wounds to the head and chest, with Schyler Henry acquiring only a couple of flesh wounds. Parrish and Longstreet escaped. Parrish was eventually hung after being convicted for another murder.

The smoke had barely cleared from the fight when Conrad Kiel dispatched a note to Helen. "Mrs. Sturd send a team and take Mr. Sturd away he is dead. C. Kiel." Helen herself went to the ranch and retrieved the body, burying Archie the next day in the four-acre family plot that would eventually inter six others.

For the next eighteen years, Helen ran the ranch on her own. Native people were always welcome on the ranch when she ran it. She loved to assist the Paiute Indians when they needed it. In 1911, the federal government decided to establish an Indian reservation in or around Las Vegas and asked for bids for the land. Whether she donated the land or was paid for it is unclear. But it was she who provided the site for today's Las Vegas Paiute Indian Colony on North Main Street.

In 1902, she signed a contract with Sen. William A. Clark of Montana and spelled out the terms for the sale of the Stewart Ranch to the San Pedro, Los Angeles and Salt Lake Railroad. This became the de facto birth certificate for the city of Las Vegas, thus making Helen one of the founding matrons of the city. The agreed price was $55,000, and did not include the Four Acres family cemetery or a small allotment of water from Las Vegas Creek. The four remaining Stewart children

133

Paranormal Investigations: The Cajun Ghost Hunter Chronicles

deeded their shares of the ranch to their mother for $1 "and love and affection," though her son Hiram, who knew only the ranching life, gave up his interest reluctantly.

Helen Stewart passed on March 16, 1926, after battling cancer. The city of Las Vegas shut down, and people came from all over to attend her funeral to pay their respects to the First Lady of Las Vegas!

I detailed this history of the Stewart ranch and the tragedy of Archie's death because the EVPs we captured during our visit were intelligent and very relevant to the circumstances surrounding the death of Stewart. After paying our admission fee and listening to a five-minute video on the history of the fort and the ranch, I acquired enough information to ask the pertinent questions of the resident spirits that were haunting the grounds. The facility occupied a city block, and there were just a couple of other people that were finishing up their tour when Barbara and I ventured out to explore.

I proceeded outside of the gate and conducted a few sessions against the wall due to the wind. I conducted a total of three three-minute sessions, and I have taken the most relevant questions and responses from each so as to exemplify the spirits surrounding us that day and the relevance of these statements to the history of the fort and the ranch.

I first asked if there was a soldier walking the grounds since there were probably soldiers at one time defending the fort. A voice replied that there was a dying soldier.

Stan: Is there a soldier walking on these grounds?
Spirit: Dying soldier!

$\triangle$: Dying Soldier

Noticing Barbara walking around the grounds and taking pictures, I asked the spirits if they knew that lady's name. I received two relevant

134

Paranormal Investigations: The Cajun Ghost Hunter Chronicles

answers: one real person's name and one spiritual person's name. A spirit responded, saying, "Barbara Ann," which is Barbara's first and middle names.

Stan: What is that lady's name that's walking these grounds?
Spirit: Barbara Ann!

︿: Barbara Ann

Another spirit gave me a response to this same question in reverse speech; however, the person's name was my mother's maiden name. This gives credence to the fact that the spirits of our loved ones surround us and follow us wherever we go.

Stan: What is that lady's name that's walking these grounds?
Spirit: Hilda Jolet!

︿: Hilda Jolet

Surprisingly, I also captured a spirit voice that said, "Stanley and Barbara find you." A spirit was probably watching us wander around the grounds with our cameras and recorders and search for spirits and was commenting on our activities!

Spirit: Stanley and Barbara find you!

︿: Find You

I asked Archibald Stewart what happened to him and if he missed his ranch. The spiritual replies were direct, intelligent, and relevant, mentioning two of the players in the tragic death of Archibald Stewart! One spirit stated that he's gonna shoot Henry, referring to Schyler Henry, and the second spirit said "Archie gunfight," which intelligently states how Archie died! A third spirit said it killed him.

135

Paranormal Investigations: The Cajun Ghost Hunter Chronicles

Stan: Archibald Stewart, what happened to you? Do you miss your ranch?
Spirit One: Gonna shoot Henry!
Spirit Two: Archie gunfight!
Spirit Three: Killed him!

‸: Archie Gunfight

I next asked Helen Stewart if she cried when Archie was killed at the Kiel ranch. One spirit responded for Archie to get back, indicative of Helen pleading with Archie not to go to the Kiel ranch. After listening to the EVP above where the spirit said that he's gonna shoot Henry, it's understandable that a spirit voice would plead for him to get back. Another spirit voice said that Helen loved him.

Stan: Helen, did you cry when Archie was killed at the Kiel ranch?
Spirit One: Archie, get back!
Spirit Two: Helen loved him!

‸: Archie, Get Back

I then received two more pleas from spirits saying, "Please, don't get in fight!" I think Helen was pleading with Archie, telling him not to shoot Schyler Henry. I think she also begged him by saying, "You don't have to shoot him." From all of these EVPs, it's evident that Archie stormed out of the house determined to go to the Kiel ranch and shoot Schyler Henry!

Spirit One: Please, don't get in fight!
Spirit Two: You don't have to shoot him!

‸: Don't Get In Fight

I asked Helen if she was sorry that she didn't get to tell Archie she loved him before he died. A spirit replied that she loved him, which was evidently Helen, and another spirit said that Henry f—cked him

Paranormal Investigations: The Cajun Ghost Hunter Chronicles

up! These spirits were definitely present when Archibald Stewart's body was recovered since this profane EVP describes a man that was shot three times.

Stan: Helen, are you sorry you didn't just get to tell Archie you loved him before he got killed?
Spirit One: I loved him!
Spirit Two: Henry f—cked him up!

‿: Henry F—cked Him Up

I will end this chapter on a more humble note than the tragedy cited above. I asked Helen Stewart if she missed the Paiute Indians that she loved and cared for after Archie's death. A spirit replied that she missed them, and another spirit said that she would assist the Paiute. A third voice was captured that asked, "Can you help us?" I assumed this was a Paiute woman begging for assistance from the always generous, loving, and caring Helen Stewart.

Stan: Helen, do you miss your Paiute Indians that you used to take care of?
Spirit One: I miss them!
Spirit Two: I would assist the Paiute.
Spirit Three: Can you help us?

‿: I Miss Them

137

XI

CRUISING EUROPE

http://www.cajunghosthunter.com/Cruising_Europe.html

After my mother's passing, my family's estate went into succession. My father worked hard all his life, but with only a tenth-grade education and his training in the army as a medical technician, we grew up poor without ever realizing it. My mom used a Sears credit card when necessary to buy clothes annually for her five children to go to school, and usually, it was hand-me-downs that helped us to get by. Fortunately, their house that they paid $12,000 for in 1953 had increased in value to where it sold for $98,000 in 2011. After paying the state for medical and nursing home care for my mother in her last two years on this earth, we each had around $10,000 as our inheritance. I used this to take Barbara on the cruise of a lifetime—Europe.

We had scheduled our trip with a reputable cruise ship company, starting in Spain then proceeding to two ports in France, three in Italy, three in Greece, and then finally back to Venice, Italy. My EVP recorder malfunctioned in France, and anything that I had captured was erased. I tried to perform several EVP sessions in Florence and Rome, but I did not capture anything worthy of sharing. However, when we got to Pompeii at the foot of Mount Vesuvius, I did capture several good EVPs, most of them involving me and my name.

In the first session, a spirit immediately made a statement about Stan still loving Hilda. My dad's name is also Stanley, so they could have been talking about either one of us.

Paranormal Investigations: The Cajun Ghost Hunter Chronicles

Spirit: Stan still loves Hilda!

‿: Stan Loves Hilda

I then asked them what my name was, and a spirit replied correctly.

Stan: What is my name?
Spirit: Stanley!

‿: Stanley

In the next session, I again asked what my name was. This time, a spirit replied that I was a godsend!

Stan: What is my name?
Spirit: A godsend!

‿: A Godsend

I captured this spirit asking what I was looking for.

Spirit: What's he looking for?

‿: What's He Looking For?

Next, I received this spirit that said that I will pray for my mother, Hilda!

Spirit: Stan will pray for Hilda!

‿: Pray for Hilda

Once again, I asked the spirits what my name was. The response was direct, intelligent, and honest!

Stan: What is my name?

142

Paranormal Investigations: The Cajun Ghost Hunter Chronicles

Spirit: We don't know your name!

︿: We Don't Know Your Name

As I was walking through the ruins of Pompeii, I took a few minutes to break away from the tour group and went to stand up against the wall of a building to perform a short session. When I started the recorder, I captured this lost soul letting me know he wasn't a ghost and he thought he was still alive!

Spirit: I'm not a ghost . . . I'm a tired old man!

︿: Tired Old Man

A spirit then said, "Talk to him, Stanley!" Were they asking me to talk to the tired old man to let him know that he was a ghost and no longer alive? Maybe they were talking to another spirit and telling them to talk to me.

Spirit: Talk to him . . . Stanley!

︿: Talk to Him, Stanley

The spirit in the previous EVP session didn't know my name, but in this session, a spirit knew that I was subcontracted to Chevron!

Spirit: He works for Chevron!

︿: He Works for Chevron

Now, most of my siblings and my parents always called me Stanley Junior since I was named after my father. A spirit said my name in this manner and then mentioned that my health was kickin'! I'm still trying to figure out if they meant that in a good way or a bad way.

Spirit: Stanley Junior's health's kickin'!

Paranormal Investigations: The Cajun Ghost Hunter Chronicles

‸: Health's Kickin'

A spirit then said that something was trying to burn them. Were they experiencing the falling lava from Pompeii and letting me know that the flying embers were trying to burn them?

Spirit: Trying to burn me!

‸: Trying to Burn Me

Finally, in this Pompeii session, I received this highly political EVP from a spirit that was making a future prediction about our freedom. Being in a nation where Obama was recently reelected president, our phones and computers are constantly tapped, and our constitutional rights are being trampled upon daily. Was this a prophecy come true?

Spirit: Y'all will never go free again!

‸: Never Go Free Again

In my final session in Pompeii, I again went and stood a little distance from the group, trying to eliminate any background noise. My first EVP was a spirit asking a question about a centaur, a creature in Greek mythology.

Spirit: How big is a centaur? We passed us a big one!

‸: How Big Is a Centaur?

A spirit then talked about how education and school will save them, and a little while later, another spirit said he was educated. I put these two together since they were related.

Spirit One: Educate! School's gonna save 'em!
Spirit Two: I'm educated!

Paranormal Investigations: The Cajun Ghost Hunter Chronicles

^: I'm Educated

I then stepped out of my bounds and directly asked the spirits how I'm going to die. A spirit then intelligently and mockingly said my name and said "That's bothering you, huh?"

Stan: How will I die?
Spirit: Stanley . . . that's bothering you, huh?

^: How Will I Die?

A spirit then warned me to not take any crap from Hilda. Were they referring to my mother? I found this very strange!

Spirit: Don't take no crap from Hilda!

^: Don't Take No Crap

The next EVP has two spirits, one saying to get off him and another saying that the tears are filling. Were they expressing their dismay at the lava covering them and the crying of tears from the victims of Vesuvius?

Spirit One: Get off of me!
Spirit Two: The tears are filling!
^: The Tears Are Filling

A spirit then said that she could not breathe in there. Was she referring to the sulfurous odor of the gases from the lava flows that inundated Pompeii?

Spirit: I cannot breathe in there!

^: I Cannot Breathe

145

Paranormal Investigations: The Cajun Ghost Hunter Chronicles

Finally, the last EVP in Pompeii is very thought-provoking and personal. A spirit said that he would rather be killed than die. Does he mean that he would rather be killed instantly than suffer a slow, painful death?

Spirit: I'd rather be killed than to die!

‸: I'd Rather Be Killed

Two days later, we were in Athens at the base of the hill leading to the Parthenon. I was standing in front of a memorial where St. Paul had preached, and I conducted a short EVP session there. In this session, a spirit immediately said when I turned the recorder on that he guessed they would light up the sky. I'm not sure what he meant by that.

Spirit: I guess we'll light up the sky.

‸: Light Up the Sky

The only other significant EVP in this session said that they wanted me dead.

Spirit: I want to see him dead!

‸: See Him Dead

The next day, we went to Mykonos, Greece. We had booked an excursion that took us to the ruins on the island of Delos. This was the most beautiful day of our cruise! The day was very hot and dry. Fortunately, there was a wind blowing on the island that made the heat bearable. Like my sessions in Pompeii, I had to separate myself from the tour group so that I could perform EVP sessions while minimizing the background noise of other people talking. When we were beginning the tour, I performed a short EVP after some introductory history by our guide. While I was following Barbara around, I asked the spirits what her name was. They replied "Barbara Ann," correctly saying her

146

Paranormal Investigations: The Cajun Ghost Hunter Chronicles

middle name. They also said to take her home. I guess they wanted her as much as I did!

Stan: What's that lady's name in the yellow shirt?
Spirit: Barbara Ann. Take her home!

⌃: Take Her Home

Using the information from the tour guide, I asked the spirits what the god Apollo represented. A spirit replied correctly!

Stan: What was Apollo the god of?
Spirit: The sun . . . see!

⌃: Apollo

Later during our walk through the ruins, I stopped behind a wall to block the wind and performed a quick session. I captured one good EVP that was very disturbing to me. The spirits knew my father was dead!

Stan: Any spirits walking here?
Spirit One: We're dead!
Spirit Two: Your father's dead!

⌃: Your Father's Dead

The next day, we were in Katakolon, Greece. We visited the site of Olympia, where the first Olympic Games were held.

After the excursion, we were brought back to the ship and were allowed a couple of hours to walk into the town for some souvenir shopping. We stopped at this Greek Orthodox church, but the doors were locked. I performed an EVP session outside as there was no one around there. I first asked if they knew my name, and a spirit, in a very clear voice with a Greek accent, answered correctly!

147

Paranormal Investigations: The Cajun Ghost Hunter Chronicles

Stan: What is my name?
Spirit: Stanley!

‸: Stanley

I picked up this spirit voice that was making a plea about someone named John killing them.

Spirit: John Curtrell killing me!

‸: Killing Me

Next, there was this girl's voice that asked me in her Greek accent to make her laugh.

Spirit: Make me laugh!

‸: Make Me Laugh

Some spirits then let me know that it wasn't good in there. How could it not be good in a church?

Spirit One: Not good . . .
Spirit Two: In here!

‸: Not Good in Here

To close out these wonderful sites in Europe where we had the best time of our lives, a spirit said something that lots of people in my life have called me in a shortened version as a nickname—"Stan the Man." However, the spirit told me using my entire first name that I was the man!

Spirit: Stanley . . . you're the man!

‸: Stanley, You're the Man!

148

Paranormal Investigations: The Cajun Ghost Hunter Chronicles

Finally, a little humor from a spirit in the stateroom of our cruise ship. We had been in the hot sun of Olympia, Greece, near Katakolon, and Barbara had a little bit of a sunburn, although due to her dark complexion, she rarely burns. That evening, she was stepping out of the bathroom after taking a shower, dressed in only a bra and panties, while I was performing an EVP in the room, and I asked the spirits if they thought she was hot. The immediate response was so clear over the headphones that I processed it so she could listen to it. We had a good laugh before going out for our last evening on board a ship.

Stan: You think she's hot?
Barbara: That's why I don't got no clothes on!
Spirit: Too sexy for my body . . . too sexy!

<u>^</u>: Too Sexy

XII

CRUISING THE CARIBBEAN

http://www.cajunghosthunter.com/Cruising_the_Caribbean.html

B arbara and I planned a weeklong cruise out of New Orleans only fifty miles from our home in August 2012. We had been gifted this cruise for purchasing membership in a vacation club and decided on this one since it went to a couple of ports in Jamaica and the Cayman Islands that we had never been before. As our cruise date approached, it was a wait-and-see situation for us boarding as Hurricane Isaac was in the Gulf of Mexico, and we were monitoring its path to see if we should leave our home. The projected path on the morning of our departure had the storm going between Mobile and Pensacola, so we decided to go. I showed our son Philip what needed to be done if the storm approached, such as boarding up the windows of our home. We boarded the ship on the Sunday afternoon of August 26.

We had to cruise for two days before we arrived at our first port of call, Montego Bay, Jamaica. While we were at sea, I was monitoring the storm's progress on my computer. Needless to say, the storm had made a dramatic turn and was going to follow a path similar to Hurricane Gustav in 2008. I was very worried as I had forgot to tell Philip that the back door in the utility room of our home had a tendency to fly open on its own due to settling of the foundation and that he needed to tie the door handle inside to the refrigerator in order to secure it. My plight was worsened by the path of the storm going directly over my hometown of Schriever, Louisiana. The storm hit on August 29, exactly seven years after Hurricane Katrina and the morning of our first excursion. Barbara and I were both jittery and worried that the

Paranormal Investigations: The Cajun Ghost Hunter Chronicles

back door wasn't secured and that the storm would blow it open, with the ensuing wind and rain destroying our home.

Our first tour stop was up in the hills with a panoramic view of the port of Montego Bay and our cruise ship. This was accompanied by the guides bringing out some jugs of homemade punch that had an ample amount of rum, which helped to calm Barbara and me down from our storm worries. The excursion then proceeded to a stop at St. Mary's Anglican Church in the parish of Saint James.

St. Mary's is located on the Montpelier Estate, and the cornerstone dates back to 1847. Old Montpelier was one of the estates burned during the great slave rebellion in the western parishes of Jamaica between 1831–1832. Constructed of cut stone, it has a pronounced pointed arch-stone architrave defining the entrance. The sides contain pointed arch windows indicative of Gothic architecture. The rear has an outstanding multipartite arch window. Formerly the slave hospital, it was the scene of a noted slave uprising and served as the local church after the rebellion.

When we arrived, all the tourists got out of our jeep-safari buses, and some went to the restrooms while others went inside the church. I decided to perform an EVP outside while everyone toured inside the building to eliminate any vocal contamination. I asked if there were any spirits there and how old they were when they died. One spirit told me his age in a clear voice with an English accent.

Stan: How old were you when you died?
Spirit: Twenty-one!

⌒: Twenty-One

I then received a spirit that told me to pray to Ms. Nellie.

Spirit: Pray to Ms. Nellie!

Paranormal Investigations: The Cajun Ghost Hunter Chronicles

^: Pray to Ms. Nellie

I then walked up to go in the church and passed a lady coming out on her way to the restrooms. I chuckled as I almost walked into her and excused myself, and a spirit said that they had seen her.

Stan: Excuse me!
Spirit: I've seen her!

^: I've Seen Her

I went into the church after the other tourists had walked around as much as they wanted and most were leaving the building. It gave me a good opportunity to conduct a quick EVP with no one talking around the altar. As I turned on the recorder, I asked if there were any slaves there. I picked up a voice saying he was a slave.

Stan: Any slaves walking here?
Spirit: Me a slave!

^: Me a Slave

My last EVP there in Jamaica reflected the temperature of the late-August dog days of summer. A spirit said it was hot.

Spirit: It's hot in here!

^: It's Hot

The next day, August 29, we were in Georgetown on Grand Cayman Island. We had a wonderful tour on a private minibus with only one other couple on board, and they booked only half of the tour. We became well acquainted with our tour guide, Leonardo Henry, on the excursion. He brought us to Seven Mile Beach and to a turtle farm. We then proceeded to a gift shop in Hell where we took some funny pictures. Our next stop was the Conch Shell House.

Paranormal Investigations: The Cajun Ghost Hunter Chronicles

In 1935, from Barker's Beach on West Bay, four thousand conch shells were hauled to the site to begin the construction of Carol Henderson's dream house. It was a slow process completing the house as sometimes the workers only were able to add thirty shells per day in building it. Mr. Henderson acquired some barrels of concrete and steel that were left over from the construction of a wireless station that had been contracted by the Cuban government, where the Government Administration Building (the Glass House) sits today. He added the roof, window, and doors after building on it for two years, and then he moved to the United States, never to return.

The house was abandoned for half a century before the Hendersons' son, Mike, refurbished it in 1973 to the appearance that it has today. Rumors have it that the house is haunted due to a Caribbean superstition that conch shells are bad luck. It stands alone on one and a half acres, 1,200 yards from the east coast of Grand Cayman. Many Caymanians tell of the house being haunted by *duppies* (ghosts), with things falling out of the cupboards and doors mysteriously slamming. The owners had a mango tree removed in 1978, thinking that it was the cause of the haunting, and supposedly, the removal worked.

Our tour guide parked the minibus in the front of the house, and we all got out and took a look around outside since it is a private residence and no inside tours are allowed. We could walk around outside all we wanted, and I proceeded to do an EVP after I heard about the duppies.

I asked if there were spirits there, and a woman told me that she needed someone to love her.

Stan: Any spirits walking here?
Spirit: I want someone to love me!

⌃: Someone to Love Me

Paranormal Investigations: The Cajun Ghost Hunter Chronicles

I next received this weird EVP by someone needing help because he blew up. The way he said it is kind of comical because of the way he inflected the word *blew*.

Spirit: Help me . . . I blew up!

⌃: Blew Up

I then captured this spirit that sensed my anxiety over leaving Philip alone to tend to the house during a hurricane while we were isolated on our vacation away from home.

Spirit: Stan wants to be near Philip!

⌃: Be near Philip

My final EVP in front of the Conch House seems related to the first EVP captured where this spirit said, "He loves you!"

Spirit: He loves you!

⌃: He Loves You

We then went to the Tortuga Rum Factory and visited the gift shop where we had free tastes of many different rums and rum cakes. I think they let you sample as much as you want because they want you to get tipsy enough to purchase a few items. Of course, I did! We then went to an outdoor flea market where there were several vendors selling native jewelry, artifacts, and clothes. Our other passengers, Liz and Randy Ayotte of Plano, Texas, then left to return to their cruise ship as their part of the tour was over.

Leonardo took Barbara and me to the East End of the island, where we stopped at a restaurant that actually was in the back of someone's house. We walked up some stairs on the side of the house where there was a small room with a few tables. We stepped up to the counter and

157

Paranormal Investigations: The Cajun Ghost Hunter Chronicles

ordered some wonderful Caribbean food that they made for us fresh in their kitchen. While waiting, Leonardo brought us outside for a short walk down the road where there was the memorial to the Wreck of the Ten Sail.

This was a historic shipwreck that occurred off the East End of Grand Cayman on February 8, 1794. There was a convoy of ten ships that wrecked on the surrounding reef while they were traveling to the United States and Britain from Jamaica. In November of 1793, the British Royal Navy had captured a twelve-pounder French frigate, *L'Inconstante*, off the coast of Saint-Domingue and renamed it the HMS *Convert*. Her seasoned captain, John Lawford, was ordered to escort a six-vessel merchant convoy from Jamaica. The convoy was joined by three other ships bound for the United States. The nine ships that sailed alongside the *Convert* were RMS *William and Elizabeth*, RMS *Moorhall*, RMS *Ludlow*, RMS *Britannia*, RMS *Richard*, RMS *Nancy*, RMS *Eagle*, RMS *Sally*, and RMS *Fortune*.

Captain Lawson had miscalculated his ship's course and thought that he had passed Grand Cayman and was heading due north to Cuba and Florida. Six merchant ships had passed him when he was called on deck to observe some breakers they were approaching. He tried to steer clear, but a merchant ship struck the *Convert* into the reef, and she was wrecked and swamped with water. The trailing ships also suffered, and the people living on the East End and Bodden Town braved the stormy waters and came to the rescue of all the passengers. Unfortunately, eight people died as a result of the shipwreck.

After his rescue, Captain Lawford sent distress messages to the governor of Havana and to his commander in chief, Commodore John Ford. After receiving Lawford's distress call, Ford sent a rescue to the shipwrecked remaining on the island. The HMS *Success* was sent to take Lawford and his crew back to Port Royal in March 1794, where he was court-martialed aboard the same ship. He was acquitted of all charges and served with distinction until he retired in 1811.

Paranormal Investigations: The Cajun Ghost Hunter Chronicles

Barbara and Leonardo walked down the beach while I positioned myself behind the memorial and performed an FM scan EVP with my RT-EVP recorder. I wasn't able to hear anything in my earphones while I was recording, but I did pick up some very clear voices over the waves when I processed the WAV file.

For my first question, I asked if any pirates were walking there and, surprisingly, received a positive response twenty seconds later mentioning pirates, so I pieced the question and answer together.

Stan: Any spirits walking here? Any pirates?
Spirit: Pirates . . . walking here!

^: Any Pirates

I then received a spirit saying that the Eliot broke. Was that one of the merchant ships that wasn't recorded in the history of the wreck? Perhaps it was another ship that was moored and whose ropes broke.

Spirit: How they know the Eliot broke?

^: Eliot Broke

I next captured this remorseful EVP when I asked if people had drowned.

Stan: Did your ship sink and you drowned?
Spirit: Too bad they drowned!

^: Too Bad

Then there was a spirit who said to saddle up. Were they possibly using horses to rescue and transport the victims of the wrecks to safety?

Spirit: Come here and saddle up!

159

Paranormal Investigations: The Cajun Ghost Hunter Chronicles

‿: Saddle Up

Finally, I had this same voice that was making statements throughout the session in forward and reverse speech. It fascinates me that the same spirit's voice is saying all the words in these phrases that tell about her being buried and that she can't be poisoned. I kept playing this over and over when I pieced it altogether, but I still can't make sense of it. The reader will definitely need headphones or earbuds to hear this over the wind and the waves in the background.

Spirit: Stay with me. Run to her while you bury me. You can't poison me. Now my boyfriend's happy!

‿: My Boyfriend's Happy

We were pressed for time after eating, so Leonardo brought us to Pedro St. James Castle and arranged for us a quick tour of the house and grounds bypassing the twenty-minute video presentation.

Dwarfing the surrounding single-level wattle-and-daub dwellings that were its neighbors in 1780, the Great House at Pedro Point towered three stories and sported stone walls eighteen inches thick. Slate was imported from England for the roof and floors while its massive size was accentuated by sweeping verandas and large shuttered windows. Due to its elaborate construction, this made the Great House the Caymanian equivalent of a European castle, and the term "Pedro Castle" is used by local residents to this day.

Because the population of the island was only five hundred in the late eighteenth century, Grand Cayman was just a little fishing village. William Eden, the landowner and farmer of the adjoining plantation, built the house using slave labor. Pedro St. James has been put to a variety of uses—including a courthouse, jail, government assembly, and restaurant—since its construction more than two centuries ago. The Castle has survived hurricanes, fires, vandalism, and rumors

Paranormal Investigations: The Cajun Ghost Hunter Chronicles

of being jinxed. Today it stands as a dynamic piece of Caymanian heritage.

On December 5, 1831, Pedro St. James was the venue for a meeting where the decision was made to form the first elected parliament. A liaison from the governor of Jamaica, Robert Thompson, was sent on May 3, 1835, and held court at Pedro St. James to issue the proclamation ending slavery in the British Empire. Thus, Pedro St. James became known as the Birthplace of Democracy in the Cayman Islands and the site where the slaves of the island were granted their freedom.

Over time, the building has been buffeted by hurricanes, struck by lightning, and engulfed by fire. The Eden family abandoned the Castle in 1877 after lightning struck the main building and killed their daughter, Mary Jane. It fell into decay, and by 1910, only the four original stone walls remained. The Hurlston family renovated it in 1914, but it was then abandoned in 1920. Thomas Hubbell purchased the property in 1959, renovated it, and lived there until 1963. The owners operated it as a restaurant and hotel from 1967, but tragedy struck in 1970 when it fell victim to a severe fire.

After reparation, it once again was operated as a restaurant from 1974 until the late 1980s when it was damaged by a hurricane and another fire. Eventually, the restaurant operation went bankrupt in 1989, and the Castle again sat vacant.

The Cayman Islands Government purchased the property in 1991 for development as an historic site. The government then retained the services of the Canadian firm of Commonwealth Historic Resource Management Limited to develop a restoration and interpretation plan for the site. That work concluded in 1996 at a cost of approximately $8 million and produced the historic site that exists today.

I took my time on entering the lower part of the house where there is a jail, kitchen, and storerooms. Barbara and Leonardo continued to

161

Paranormal Investigations: The Cajun Ghost Hunter Chronicles

tour other parts of the house and grounds as I started an EVP session in the jail. The jail had a wax figure sitting on a bed and was very creepy when I first entered it. I started the recorder, and immediately the spirits said my name. Ten seconds later, they said that I was best of the cream. Notice the full-toned Caribbean accent of the last spirit when he says Stanley!

Spirit One: You are Stanley!
Spirit Two: Best of the cream!
Spirit Three: Stanley!

^: Best of the Cream

I asked if there were any spirits in the jail, and a spirit replied that his name was Tom and that he was a prisoner. He said it in both the forward and reverse speech in the EVP captured.

Stan: Any spirits walking here?
Spirit Forward: Here Prison Tom!
Spirit Reversed: Tom prisoner here!

^: Tom Prisoner

In response to the same question, a spirit said he was Old John and that he was a spook. It's funny how some spirits express the fact that they are a ghost.

Stan: Any spirits walking here?
Spirit: Old John, the spook, is here!

^: Old John, the Spook

Next, I surprisingly received this spirit voice who must be a New Orleans Saints fan. Our Saints' popularity has a far-reaching effect on fans, even the spirits of the Cayman Islands!

162

Paranormal Investigations: The Cajun Ghost Hunter Chronicles

Spirit: Who Dat!

^: Who Dat

I went up to the second floor where the smart dining room, court, and the veranda were located. I performed another EVP session up there while walking around. I first picked up a spirit that said that Satan's following her.

Spirit: Satan's a-following me!

^: Satan

I then received this spirit that said her Alfredo was dead.

Spirit: My Alfredo's dead in here!

^: Alfredo's Dead

Next, a spirit said that it was crazy in there. Were they referring to the courtroom?

Spirit: It's crazy in here!

^: Crazy in Here

Being that I was near the courtroom, perhaps I was picking up residual voices from past crimes that had been committed. I captured this EVP where a spirit said that Louis maimed someone's eye.

Spirit: Louis maimed his eye!

^: Louis Maimed

A spirit then said that somehow the bells were ringing. I wonder what type of bell was ringing and for what reason?

163

Paranormal Investigations: The Cajun Ghost Hunter Chronicles

Spirit: Somehow, the bells are ringing!

͡: Bells Ringing

I then picked up this spirit where the forward and reverse speeches were related, so I pieced them together. It's a disturbing EVP talking about a kid killing his mom, how he's Howard's kid, and how Howard killed him. Did Howard kill his kid for killing his wife?

Spirit Forward: Your kid killed his mom!
Spirit Reverse: Howard's kid . . . he killed him!

͡: Howard's Kid

I proceeded up the stairs to the living quarters on the third floor. I started an EVP session outside of the nursery where the children from the Eden family were struck by lightning. I asked the spirits once again what my name was, and they responded with a Caribbean dialect.

Stan: What is my name?
Spirit: Stanley

͡: Stanley

This spirit named Nurse Nellie told me not to mess with her. Was she the family's nurse or nanny and was warning me? How coincidental that I was in the nursery when this was captured.

Spirit: I'm Nurse Nellie. Don't you mess with me!

͡: Nurse Nellie

Next, I had this spirit that addressed Nurse Nellie and told her his name was Monk.

Spirit: Hello, Ms. Nellie, I'm Monk!

164

Paranormal Investigations: The Cajun Ghost Hunter Chronicles

⌃: Monk

There was then a woman's voice that stated that her baby was dead, and then a little while later, there was another woman's voice that said her baby turned green. Was this the same woman, and was she the mother of the little girl that was killed by lightning?

Spirit: Baby's dead! Ah, my baby turned green!

⌃: Baby's Dead

I went downstairs to join Barbara and Leonardo, and they were in the yard under some trees that Leonardo had climbed to bring down the savory fruit for Barbara to enjoy. We then got back in the minibus and were brought back to the port to catch the boat back to the cruise ship. Grand Cayman is the jewel of the Caribbean, and I highly recommend it to anyone for its wonderful beaches and its rich history. I definitely plan to return in the fall of 2013 during Pirate's Week, their annual festival, and hope to be escorted by Leonardo once more.

XIII

PATRICK DRIVE AND THE HELMS' GARAGE

http://www.cajunghosthunter.com/Patrick_Dr_Helm_s_Garage.html

L ike all ghost hunters, I decided to use my equipment at my house to see if any paranormal activity was occurring. We were friends with the former owners of my house, Sue and Kenny Helms, since we had lived in the house next door to them for a number of years. Their daughter, Kathy, was friends with my daughter, Melissa, so we got to know the family over the years.

In 1999, Barbara and I purchased their property and garage apartment where they lived after Mr. Kenny had died, and Ms. Sue had moved to a house near Calumet, Louisiana. We put a double-wide in the field where Mr. Kenny used to grow his garden, and both of my daughters lived in the garage apartment off and on throughout the years.

In 2008, Hurricane Gustav hit, and the eye of the storm passed over Schriever. We had evacuated to Hot Springs, Arkansas, and were unable to return to our residence until five days after the storm hit. Once we returned, the storm had damaged our trailer's roof and the roof of the apartment. We repaired the trailer, but the garage apartment was uninsured and in such disarray that we left it alone. Eventually, I had to raze the apartment on the top and put a roof over the ground floor where the workshop and garage were located.

On Mother's Day of May 8, 2011, my kids had come over with their children, and I was talking about the new RT-EVP recorder that I had acquired where I could talk to spirits. Well, the children were all captivated by the thought of talking to ghosts, so they wanted me to

Paranormal Investigations: The Cajun Ghost Hunter Chronicles

perform an EVP session with them in the Helms' garage where Mr. Kenny used to work in his shop and also where he would distill his muscadine wine.

I let the kids know that even though we would ask questions, we wouldn't hear the answers until I processed the files since human ears can't hear at the noise levels that the spirits speak. I asked the usual questions, such as if there were any spirits there and what were their names. I didn't capture any good responses to the questions. One of my granddaughter's friends, Haley, wanted me to tell Mr. Kenny hi for her. When I did, he gave her a most gracious response!

Stan: Haley says hi! Can you tell her hi, Mr. Kenny? Hello?
Spirit: I think you're pretty, girl!

$\triangle$: Pretty Girl

Three days later, I was performing an EVP session during a thunderstorm, hoping that the electrical activity would get the spirits talking. When I asked if the lightning scared them, a spirit pleaded for protection!

Stan: Does that lightning scare y'all?
Spirit: Hurt me or protect me . . . Ow!

$\triangle$: Protect Me

Later that year on November 6, 2011, the kids had come by and wanted to do a session in the garage. During the session, Jacob had asked Mr. Kenny a question, and I asked him if he knew who that little boy was. He answered correctly.

Stan: Mr. Kenny, you know that little boy's name that just asked that question?
Spirit: Jacob!

Paranormal Investigations: The Cajun Ghost Hunter Chronicles

^: Jacob

On November 18, 2011, I decided to go to the Oaks, the nursing home where my mom passed, and try to perform an EVP in the room where she died. It was the anniversary of her death, and I felt that I would be able to communicate with her in the room where her soul left this earth. I was not disappointed. I convinced her former roommate, Ms. Bernadette Breaux, that I wanted to record us trying to contact my mother, and she agreed. I asked Hilda to tell Bernadette that she loved her, and a spirit said that she loved Bernadette!

Stan: Mama, tell Ms. Bernadette that you love her.
Spirit: I love Bernadette!

^: Love Bernadette

Now during this session, Ms. Bernadette asked me to get her the glass of water that was on her mobile tray and pass it to her so she could take a sip. She thanked me, and I put it back. I then captured this spirit that mimicked me handing Ms. Bernadette the water to drink!

Spirit: Stan . . . water! Thank you!

^: Water

Later in this same session, I was explaining to Ms. Bernadette that since spirits no longer have their bodies, the voices one hears probably won't sound like they did in real life. However, I let her know that it's what they say that helps you to identify if you're talking to your loved one that you are trying to contact. After I told her that my mom always called me Stanley Junior, ten seconds later, a spirit said that she loved me and called me Stanley Junior!

Stan: When I hear Stanley Junior . . .
Ms. Bernadette: Uh huh?
Stan: You know who it is!

171

Paranormal Investigations: The Cajun Ghost Hunter Chronicles

Ms. Bernadette: Yeah!
Spirit: I love Stanley Junior.

︿: I Love Stanley Junior.

My brother-in-law, Harold Chauvin, had just been released from jail in September of that year after being incarcerated for three years. Harold is a Vietnam veteran who had been arrested for several DUIs in the past. He has PTSD like many of the vets who returned from Vietnam who dull the psychological pain from combat with alcohol or drugs. He was living with us as he readjusted to life outside of prison until he could afford a place of his own. We dearly love Harold and will do anything to help him anytime, anywhere.

On November 28, 2011, I performed an EVP session in my bedroom in front of a picture of Harold's father, Gordon Chauvin, and I asked him what his son's name was who was living with me. A spirit told me that they treasure him and that I should feed him and hug him.

Stan: Gordon, what's your son's name living with me right now?
Spirit: Harold! We treasure him! Feed him! Hug him!

︿: We Treasure Him

On December 28, 2011, while Barbara was working, I had some free time on my hands, so I decided to go in the bedroom and perform an EVP session in front of the vanity that used to belong to my mom and where Barbara had placed pictures of her mom and dad. There is a bronze Pietà that sits on the vanity in front of the pictures. The Pietà was a gift from the funeral home and was on a corner of one of the caskets for Barbara's parents. At the time, I thought the statue was from Gordon's casket and asked him if he liked it. The answer was astounding and truly amazing!

Stan: Gordon, I'll bet you love these Pietàs that were on your casket, huh?
Spirit: It's Marguerite's casket the statue's from!

Paranormal Investigations: The Cajun Ghost Hunter Chronicles

‿: Pietà

When I processed this EVP and realized that I may have been mistaken, I asked Barbara when she got home whose casket the Pietà was from. She replied that it was from Marguerite's casket! An intelligent spirit had corrected me on my mistake! Since this capture was very faint and the clarity will be lost with overlaying and uploading from my computer to my server, if the reader can't hear it properly with headphones or earbuds, please e-mail me at stanleyjolet@cajunghosthunter.com, and I will e-mail the file back to you.

Later in that same session, I asked Marguerite to tell Barbara that she loved her. A spirit replied that she failed Barbara horribly! Dr. Dave Oester with the International Ghost Hunter's Society claims that spirits become earthbound due to guilt and feelings that they didn't get the chance to reconcile before passing to the other side. Was this the spirit of Marguerite professing some guilt that she carried with her about Barbara?

Stan: Marguerite, tell your daughter you love her.
Spirit: I have failed Barbara horribly!

‿: Failed Barbara

On January 6, 2012, I performed another EVP in my bedroom with Harold and asked Gordon how he knew that the Pietàs were from Marguerite's casket and if he was at the funeral since he had died a couple of years before she did.

Stan: How did you know that? Were you at the funeral with us?
Spirit: A priest!

‿: A Priest

173

Paranormal Investigations: The Cajun Ghost Hunter Chronicles

Harold then asked his daddy about the upcoming New Orleans Saints game and if he thought the Saints were going to win. The spirit's answer was about what every young boy would do with his daddy on a Sunday afternoon in Cajun country when growing up.

Harold: And what about that Saints game? You think the Saints gonna win?
Gordon: Just grew up with me watching them!

△: Saints Game

Five seconds later, I captured this stunning EVP verifying who the spirit was that was speaking in the previous EVP!

Spirit: Think about it. Harold and Barbara's Paw!

△: Harold and Barbara's Paw

Now, Gordon's brother N. J. Chauvin was very dear to both Gordon and Harold. I met NJ once after Barbara and I had married, and he had a playful sense of humor, like his brother Gordon. All the relatives loved him, and everyone sadly missed him after he passed. I proceeded to ask Gordon if he and NJ were in heaven, and Harold interjected to tell him hi if he was.

Stan: Hey, Gordon, is Uncle NJ up there with y'all in heaven?
Harold: If he is, tell him I said hi!
Spirit: NJ could feel me . . . go back! Wake up!

△: Wake Up

To this day, I can't figure out what the spirit meant to go back and wake up, but the truly amazing part of this response is that immediately after asking our questions, an intelligent spirit had mentioned NJ in such a rich, deep voice! I still don't know what he meant about "NJ could feel me." Perhaps in his last days, Gordon was communicating with his

174

Paranormal Investigations: The Cajun Ghost Hunter Chronicles

relatives that had crossed over, and NJ could sense or feel that Gordon was going to need his guidance and help to cross over to the other side. I will talk more about that later.

The last EVP from this session had to be Barbara's mom and dad speaking of Barbara leaving her first husband. I won't go into details, but she had been physically abused, and like many battered women, she had stayed for as long as she could bear it because she was raising three young children. Barbara is a very strong person, with a will unlike any other person that I've ever met, and when she decides that she's had enough of something, that is it. She will close that door never to be reopened and push forward with a new life and fresh attitude.

This EVP names Barbara, tells of her being wounded, and then calls her a sweetheart. Next, it sounds like they are coaxing her to "do it," and then they say that "she walked out"!

Spirit: Barbara Ann, he had wounded her, that sweetheart! Do it! She walked out!

‿: She Walked Out

On March 10, 2012, I went into the Helms' garage and performed an EVP. Now, both Mr. Kenny and Ms. Sue loved to smoke cigarettes. They both liked to drink, especially the muscadine wine that they would ferment in their garage, and enjoyed a good cigarette while they indulged in their libations. I asked Mr. Kenny if he would like a cigarette and received a positive response.

Stan: Would you like a cigarette, Mr. Kenny?
Spirit: It would . . . take puff!
Spirit: Pack it, light it!

‿: Pack It, Light It

Paranormal Investigations: The Cajun Ghost Hunter Chronicles

On May 5, 2012, inside the Helms' garage, I performed an EVP with FM scan and asked my mother if she would like some heavenly hash since she liked that more than the pralines she made when she was alive. A spirit replied that it would be wonderful!

Stan: Boy, wouldn't some heavenly hash be good right now?
Spirit: That'd be wonderful!

⌃: Wonderful

There was a violent thunderstorm on July 20, 2012, that caused the power to go out in the house, so I decided to perform an EVP session in my bedroom. At the beginning of the session, I picked up a spirit that said he wanted a monkey. There is a reason for the spirit to say this. My miniature poodle, Froo Froo, had this little pink monkey that he liked for me to throw from the living room into the kitchen for him. After he would pick it up, I would chase him from the kitchen, through the dining room, and back into the living room again. While chasing him, I would shout out at him that "I want that monkey!" This spirit was mimicking my antics whenever I chased Froo Froo with that monkey!

Spirit: I want that monkey!

⌃: I Want That Monkey

Once again, like a previous EVP in front of Gordon's picture on the vanity, I asked Gordon if he liked the Pietà from Marguerite's casket. I received a response for Gordon to bring Gordon home. What was striking about this EVP is that when Barbara got home that evening from work, I asked her what was the name of Gordon's daddy. Like I suspected, she told me his name was Gordon. So the spirit was telling Gordon to bring his son, also named Gordon, home. This is like the song "Swing Low, Sweet Chariot" where the chariot is "coming for to carry me home." Gordon's daddy came to take him home. How

Paranormal Investigations: The Cajun Ghost Hunter Chronicles

comforting to know that our loved ones are waiting to greet us and welcome us on the other side.

Stan: Gordon, do you like this Pietà from Marguerite's casket?
Spirit: Gordon, bring Gordon home!

⌃: Bring Gordon Home

Now we come to the highlight of this EVP session. My son Philip was dearly loved by my mother who was not only a retired nurse but was also a lab technician in the army during World War II. Since Philip had fought in Operation Iraqi Freedom and was a mortars expert stationed in Samarra, he had a special place in her heart because of the drastic effects that war had on Philip's psyche, leaving him with 100 percent disability due to PTSD. I have had a spirit call me by my first name, but not one spirit up to that point in time had ever pronounced my last name. There are not many people alive that can pronounce my last name correctly without me telling them how to say it first for them. Phonetically, it is pronounced Row-bless-key. This spirit was not only intelligent and answered my question but correctly pronounced our last name!

Stan: What's the name of that boy in the room across the . . . on the other side of the house? What's his name?
Spirit: That's Philip Wroblewski

⌃: Philip Wroblewski

I performed another EVP in my bedroom on August 4, 2012, and captured this spirit that said Philip was a good man.

Spirit: Philip is a good man!

⌃: Philip Is a Good Man

Paranormal Investigations: The Cajun Ghost Hunter Chronicles

The next day, Barbara decided that she wanted me to perform an EVP while we were sitting in the living room. I immediately grabbed my recorder as this was a rare occurrence for Barbara to request a session. She asked the spirits to go pet Froo Froo, who was standing in the middle of the floor, and the spirits replied that he was one "ever-living puppy" and to "pet him, son." Then, another spirit said that Mother would let him come if he pet him! I hope he's an "ever-living puppy" so that I can still cuddle with him on the other side!

Barbara: Go pet Froo Froo.
Spirit One: One ever-living puppy . . . pet him, son!
Spirit Two: Mother would let me come if I pet him!

⌢: Ever-Living Puppy

The other EVP that I captured in this session most definitely is my mother, and I'll explain why. My family on my mother's side has a history of diabetes and strokes. My great-grandmother on my grandmother's side had diabetes. My great uncle and my grandmother's brother, Wylie, died from diabetes, as did his son, Walter, when he was only in his fifties. Now, my mother dearly loved her grandmother Marie Leblanc Daigle. She even once told me that she had loved her more than her own mother!

My mother had lived in New York City when my father was stationed overseas in France during World War II, and they moved back down here after the war. They both worked for the doctors at the Ellender Clinic: Ernest, Willard, and Allen. My mom was an LPN, and my dad was the X-ray tech. When my great-grandmother had a series of strokes, my mother and father would get off work, pick up their three children at my grandmother's house, and my mother would go take care of her grandmother while my father went home with the kids. When her grandmother died, it had a profound effect on my mother, which is why this EVP is heartbreaking!

Spirit: Her death really got me! I loved her!

178

Paranormal Investigations: The Cajun Ghost Hunter Chronicles

‸: I Loved Her

It has been said that the spirits of our loved ones are most active around holidays and birthdays. During my birthday on November 7, 2012, I was home alone and decided to have a birthday EVP session. Once again, I went into my bedroom, and while I had one hand on this bust of the Sacred Heart of Jesus that my mother had given me before she died, I conducted that session. My mother dearly loved her sister Althea, who everyone called Blondie because of the color of her hair. They were close to each other in age and used to double-date and attend dances together. They would go to dances at the American Legion Hall in Houma, Louisiana, while their mother sat in a car with my grandfather and waited for them. They were close, and Aunt Blondie and her husband, Lee, were the godparents of my oldest brother, Peter.

Stan: Mama, how old were you when you died?
Spirit: I loved Aunt Blondie.

‸: I Loved Aunt Blondie

Later in this session, I asked my mother who her grandson was who was on the other side of the house, and the response from the spirit actually sounds like my Aunt Blondie! She said that the boy is mine, and then another spirit told her that the man is Philip. Then the spirit said Philip's first name and his middle name and spoke of fun things. Philip spends all day playing role-playing and first-person-shooter games on his computer. He also collects and is surrounded by action figures. Are they talking about these as his fun things?

Stan: What is your grandson's name on the other side of the house?
Spirit One: That boy is Stanley Junior's!
Spirit Two: That man is Philip! Fun-things Philip Jude!

‸: That Man Is Philip

179

Paranormal Investigations: The Cajun Ghost Hunter Chronicles

In the final EVP that I captured during this session, I told my mom that I loved her and I missed her. She then said, "I love him!"

Stan: I love you and I miss you!
Spirit: I love him!

⌃: I Love Him

I want to diverge from this treatise about my house hauntings as I have to relate a couple of paranormal experiences away from the home that were very unique to me. On November 17, 2012, Harold and I went to the LSU-Ole Miss (University of Mississippi) football game on the LSU campus. Every time we go to a game on campus, we park behind the International Cultural Center because it's free parking (although it's about a mile walk to the stadium). We usually arrive five hours early and tailgate in the truck until an hour before game time. On this particular day, the game started at 2:30 PM, so we were there at 10:15 AM in our usual spot by the lakes. I performed a P-SB7 Spirit Box session while we were waiting for the game and received some very intelligent responses. In this first video clip, I asked the spirits who the mascot is for LSU, and two spirits each said "Tiger" correctly!

Stan: This is LSU! What's their mascot?
Spirit One: Tiger!
Spirit Two: Tiger!
Stan: Tigers! That's right! LSU Tigers!

⌃: Tigers

Later in the session, I asked the spirits what my name was, and they said "Stan." When I asked the spirits how they died, they proceeded to mention my son Philip and told me to help him. Seeing that they were making statements concerning Philip, I pursued this line of questioning. I asked them the name of my son at home to see if they would respond again. They not only correctly answered Philip but also said his middle name, Jude! They subsequently asked me to help him.

180

Paranormal Investigations: The Cajun Ghost Hunter Chronicles

Let me elaborate on this session. Due to his PTSD from his Operation Iraqi Freedom deployment, Philip has been undergoing pharmaceutical treatment from the Veteran's Administration for several years now. I have assumed the responsibility of his daily financial and medical needs as his power of attorney. He has been hospitalized for his condition twice, but the only hospitals with beds for vets needing psychiatric treatment in the state of Louisiana are in Alexandria (two hundred miles away), which has twenty-eight, and Shreveport (three hundred miles away), with twelve. In fact, I had a ticket for Philip to go to the game, but he decided not to come with us that day since he wasn't in the mood to interact with a large crowd (a symptom of his condition). There is a new VA hospital that is opening in New Orleans in 2014, and perhaps the spirits were reminding me to bring him for help since this resource will soon be available.

Stan: What's my name?
Spirit: Stan!
Stan: How'd y'all die?
Spirit: Philip . . . help him!
Stan: What's my son's name that's not with us today? He's at home.
Spirit: Philip!
Stan: Philip!
Spirit: Jude!
Stan: Jude! That's right, Philip Jude!
Spirit: Philip . . . Help him!

⌃: Philip, Help Him

Later that month on November 23, which was the day after Thanksgiving, Harold and I were watching LSU play Arkansas on television. I realized that it was the sixteen-year anniversary of Gordon's death and told Harold that we should do an EVP since Gordon's spirit might be active. My instincts were correct. I asked Gordon if he was with Marguerite, and a spirit answered by saying her name.

Paranormal Investigations: The Cajun Ghost Hunter Chronicles

Stan: Gordon, are you with Marguerite now?
Spirit: Marguerite!

‿: Marguerite

Harold asked his daddy how he was doing and if he was OK over there. The spirit answered, calling out Harold's name, and said he was just right and he'd be OK.

Harold: How're you doing, Daddy? Are you OK over there?
Spirit: Harold, I'm just right! I'll be OK!

‿: I'll Be OK

The final EVP of the session is a real mindblower! Harold told both his parents that he loved them and that he missed them. Since we can't hear them in real time, the response was so surreal because they must know that I have to process an EVP before we hear them. They wanted me to give him this message that they miss him and love him.

Harold: And I love ya'll and I miss ya'll.
Spirits: Tell him . . . that I miss him today and to give him my love!

‿: Give Him My Love

On December 19, 2012, which was the fourteen-year anniversary of my father's death, I decided to do an EVP in my bedroom. I didn't get any responses related to him, but I did get three that were related to my mother. In the first one, she let me know that they were back with Aunt Odessa. Odessa was her oldest sister, who lived to be ninety-three years old, and she used to live down the street from the family. One thing I remember is that Aunt Odessa made the best pecan cakes. She would bake the cake layers, and my mother would prepare the frosting. When the cake layers were ready, Aunt Dessa would call mama on the phone to go down there, and they would put the cake together. I have that recipe, and it is definitely the best cake ever!

182

Paranormal Investigations: The Cajun Ghost Hunter Chronicles

Spirit: We're back with Aunt Odessa!

‿: Back with Aunt Odessa

I put the next two EVPs captured in this session together since I think they were related to the time when my mother was in the nursing home. The first one stated that they had a Popsicle over there, which were one of the confections that the aids distributed for their afternoon snacks. In the second one, the spirit stated that the bed was horrible. I know that one of the beds that she stayed in literally broke, and she and the mattress actually fell out of the frame. The staff had to get her a new bed!

Spirit One: I had Popsicle over here.
Spirit Two: The bed was horrible!

‿: Bed Was Horrible

My son Benjamin had driven down here from South Carolina with his daughter, Adina, over the Christmas holidays. I had not seen Adina in over two years, and this was only the third opportunity that I had to spend time with her since her birth because of the long distance from our home. My oldest brother and his wife, Peter and Debra Wroblewski, had given Ben a generous Christmas present because he had just retired from the navy and was looking for work. Ben had used some of that gift to drive down only because of Pete and Debbie's generosity, and for that I am forever grateful.

When Benjamin had gone to the store one day, I was babysitting Adina and decided to perform an EVP session with her. In this session, I caught one EVP with voices from the spirits saying that Hilda cries. Perhaps she was crying because she wasn't alive to cherish her great-granddaughter.

Spirit: Hilda . . . you cry!

Paranormal Investigations: The Cajun Ghost Hunter Chronicles

⌃: Hilda, You Cry

I had wanted to bring Benjamin to the Jolet tomb while he was down here because I knew that his presence would provide a great trigger for my mother's responses as you already know about the soft spot in her heart for our men in uniform. Ben is a skeptic, even after viewing all the evidence that I have posted on my Facebook page. On New Year's Eve, while he was getting ready to go out and enjoy the festivities before leaving the next day, I talked him into performing an EVP session with me in the living room. He asked my mother if it was all right over there, and she responded to give him a big hug from her!

Ben: Is it all right over there?
Spirit: Big hug from me!

⌃: Big Hug

Of course, I had to ask her if she wanted some pizza. On Saturday afternoons while my mother was in the nursing home, I would usually cook lunch and bring my mother a home-cooked meal for her supper so she could have a break from the cafeteria food. Sometimes she would ask me to buy her a pizza. We would always share her pizza with her roommate, Bernadette Breaux. She would let Ms. Bernadette know in advance to cancel her supper delivery with the nurses' aides because we were having pizza for supper. That is what makes this EVP so relevant.

Stan: Wouldn't you like some pizza?
Spirit: I want pizza, Bernadette!

⌃: Pizza, Bernadette

On January 13, 2013, my brother Danny Wroblewski, who lives in North Carolina, posted a picture on his Facebook page of a potato salad made in a bowl that my mother had given him, and he said that our mother loved this version of his potato salad best. I begged to differ

Paranormal Investigations: The Cajun Ghost Hunter Chronicles

with him on that since my mother had never put olives in her potato salad and I doubted that she would like it. So I told him that next time I was "spiritually online," I would ask her if she liked it. Here's her response to my question about that potato salad that I captured on January 18, 2013, in my bedroom.

Stan: Mama, Danny said that you love his potato salad with his olives in it. Do you like that potato salad?
Spirit: Not sure! I don't care. I never do. I can cook!

^: I Can Cook

On January 18, 2013, I went in the Helms' garage and performed an EVP session with my RT-EVP recorder and a spirit box session with the P-SB7. The best EVP that I captured in the EVP session spoke of the spirits praying for my mother because she was dead. During her lifetime, my mother helped many of her friends and their families in their last days because of her background as a nurse. Watching her tenderness and compassion in her friends' hour of need is something I will remember and cherish always.

Spirit: Holy saints! Your mother helped me! We prayed 'cause Hilda's dead!

^: Hilda's Dead

After the recorded EVP session, I plugged the RT-EVP recorder into my Auxio speaker and recorded the session with my Kodak camera as the recorder scanned FM frequencies in real time. I do this without using the record function on the recorder because the volume is greatly diminished if I record on it simultaneously. This way, I essentially have a spirit box scanning at fifty milliseconds, which is four times faster than the P-SB7 without the loud background noise.

I told my mother that it was me. I received responses from a male spirit voice that said "He hugged me" and that he needed help.

185

Paranormal Investigations: The Cajun Ghost Hunter Chronicles

Stan: Hello, Mama, it's Stanley Junior.
Spirit: He hugged me. I need help!

⌃: He Hugged Me

I then asked her how old she was when she died. A spirit responded, saying my mother's maiden name! She then responded that she was ninety years old, which was her age when she died!

Stan: How old were you when you died?
Spirit One: Hilda Jolet
Spirit Two: Ninety years old!

⌃: Ninety Years Old

During this session, which was only three minutes long, I picked up these EVPs that I feel are related, so I pasted them together. Previously, I mentioned how my mother dearly loved her grandmother and had to care for her after a series of strokes. These are very disheartening as you can first hear the spirit say that her grandma's death was real bad; secondly, she lamented the loss of her grandma, and finally, she told me (or Stanley Senior) that she felt depressed. Was this my mother telling me once again how she suffered because of the loss of her grandmother Marie Leblanc Daigle?

Spirit: Your grandma's death was real bad!
Spirit: Oh, my grandma!
Spirit: Stanley, I feel depressed!

⌃: Feel Depressed

I then proceeded with a P-SB7 Spirit Box session. I captured several good EVPs; however, the noise from the sweeps was too loud to post most of them. However, I did capture this one that is pretty clear. I asked my mother who was her roommate when she was in the nursing home. She responded "Bernadette" correctly!

186

Paranormal Investigations: The Cajun Ghost Hunter Chronicles

Stan: What was the name of your roommate in the nursing home?
Spirit: Bernadette.
Stan: Bernadette? That's right!

⌃: Bernadette

We were babysitting my grandchildren on January 31, 2013, when my oldest granddaughter, Aleah, decided that she wanted to ghost hunt in my bedroom with her siblings, Dylan and Jayden. We grabbed the camera, the spirit box, and the EVP recorder and proceeded to the bedroom. I first set up the recorder, and we performed an EVP session. Aleah asked her great-grandmother what her name was and received a positive response.

Aleah: Mawmaw Chauvin, what is your first name?
Spirit: Marguerite!

⌃: Marguerite

I then captured this profound message from a spirit addressing it to my sister, Pat (Patricia Beacom). It said that God was into me, and the reverse speech said that they were going to stay with God! Was this my mother saying that they were leaving their boundaries here on earth and traversing to the light to be with God? How comforting it was to me to hear that they had found God, whoever they were.

Spirit Forward Speech: God is into Stanley, Pat!
Spirit Reverse Speech: Pat, we're going to stay with God!

⌃: Stay with God

On Saint Patrick's Day on March 17, 2013, as I was reading my Facebook page, I realized that it was Kathy Helms's birthday! I immediately grabbed my EVP recorder and went out to the Helms' garage. I told Barbara on the way out the house that since it was

187

Paranormal Investigations: The Cajun Ghost Hunter Chronicles

Kathy's birthday that I might get some good responses from spirits in the garage. Once again, my instincts were correct!

I started the session by letting Mr. Kenny and Ms. Sue know that it was Kathy's birthday, and I received a response in forward and reverse speech that said that they would like to give her a hug and some money.

Stan: Ms. Sue and Mr. Kenny, it's Kathy's birthday. Wish her a happy birthday!
Spirit: We'd love to give her birthday hug! I would love to give her money!

⌃: Love to Give Her Money

In closing my presentation on the Helms' garage and my house, I have posted these two videos showing the orbs that have been captured in each. On September 9, 2011, I captured these two orbs in the garage while trying to contact Mr. Kenny.

Stan: Mr. Kenny, are you here?
Stan: Do you miss Kathy? She loves you!

⌃: Helms' Garage Orbs 09-09-11

When I performed the EVPs with my grandchildren on January 31, 2013, we also had the IR camera on during the session. In seven minutes, we captured about seven orbs, which I pasted together in the order that they appeared along with the text of the conversation inserted.

Aleah: Mawmaw Chauvin, what is your first name?
Aleah: Pawpaw Chauvin, what is your first name?
Stan: Where's my dog at? Where's my Froo Froo?
Aleah: Found him.
Stan: There he is. Froo Froo. Froo Froo's a fun dog! Show yourself!

Paranormal Investigations: The Cajun Ghost Hunter Chronicles

Stan: Show yourself! Show yourself to Aleah!
Stan: That's enough, I guess. Let's go!

⌂: 209 Patrick Drive Orbs 01-31-13

If you look closely after Aleah asks Pawpaw Chauvin what his name is, you will see the orb forming in the wall above the TV set before it shoots out past the camera. This is very convincing as it not only goes a certain direction while forming but also changes its direction and travels past the camera.

I have presented lots of evidence that were captured at my house and in the Helms' garage. I have many EVPs from my residence, far too many to put in this book, but I may make a compilation at a later date and publish those for the readers' enjoyment.

XIV

114 ADOUE STREET, HOME OF HILDA WROBLEWSKI

http://www.cajunghosthunter.com/114_Adoue_Street.php

After my mother died on November 18, 2010, we had to start the secession of her estate. It took a while for my sister to get everything in order so that we could eventually sell my mother's house on 114 Adoue Street in Houma, Louisiana. Her son and my nephew, Randy Hawthorne, had lived there for a couple of years after my mother had gone into the nursing home. That way, the home and property could be kept up to living standards.

On August 10, 2011, I had gone by the house and visited with my nephew, Randy, since he was going to be moving out and I wanted to assess what I would need to clean up in the house for the new owners. Randy is somewhat a skeptic on my paranormal work, but he agreed to let me perform an EVP session with him in the living room on that day.

During the session, I picked up a couple of intelligent EVPs. In the first one, I asked my mom if she would like to pet Randy's cat that he was holding as I was performing the EVP. A spirit responded that she petted him!

Stan: Mama, you want to pet this little, bitty kitty cat?
Spirit: I petted him!

‿: I Petted Him

The second quality EVP that I captured in this session is very compelling and intelligent. When I told my mother that she would

193

Paranormal Investigations: The Cajun Ghost Hunter Chronicles

have some new people living there and asked if she was going to miss Randy, she said that I could see her!

Stan: Mama, you're gonna have some new people living here pretty soon. You're gonna miss Randy?
Spirit: Stanley Junior sees me!

͡: Stanley Junior Sees Me

On August 26, 2011, I went to the house to see if Randy had moved and if there was anything that I needed to bring to my house that he left behind. While there, I conducted a quick session. Randy's dad, Harvey Hawthorne, had died from a massive heart attack at the age of sixty. My mother had loved her son-in-law. He used to bring her ducks and speckled trout that she thoroughly enjoyed. During Michael Jordan's last season of playing basketball, Harvey had gone to a game with friends to watch him play in New Orleans, and on the way back, he rode in the backseat and fell asleep. When his friends went to wake him up, they found he had died from a heart attack. In this EVP, you can hear a female spirit say that Harvey is with her.

Spirit: Harvey is with me!

͡: Harvey Is with Me

I went back to the house on August 29, 2011, to clean the house and to say my final good-byes. I did a thorough cleaning, and then I proceeded to perform some FM scan and ambient EVPs. I didn't capture too many and only a few with clarity in one session of an FM scan.

In this scan, I first captured this reverse speech at the twenty-two-second mark that said I was a faggot.

Spirit: He's a faggot!

͡: He's a Faggot

Paranormal Investigations: The Cajun Ghost Hunter Chronicles

Immediately after that exhortation at the twenty-four-second mark, I captured an EVP that disputed the previous spirit's claim and said that I was a good man. Was this my mother letting her feelings be known to that other spirit?

Spirit: A good man, Stanley!

⌒: A Good Man

A minute later, I captured this forward/reverse speech EVP that was very disturbing. My father, in the last eight years of his life, was in the middle stages of Alzheimer's disease. My mother was able to care for him, but occasionally, he would argue with her and have fits of rage, as most patients exhibit when they reach the later stages. My mother always portrayed strength of character whenever my sister, Pat, or I would visit them or deliver their groceries. Perhaps this spirit, if my mother, was expressing her fears she experienced while watching my father in one of his rages. In this EVP, the spirit said that Stanley's going to kill her and her face will look bad.

Spirit: Stanley's going to kill me! My face will look bad!

⌒: Stanley's Going to Kill Me

I had three ambient sessions over there where I captured some data but cannot determine the relevancy to the location. Perhaps they were residual from next door since my mother had some neighbors that were noisy and had a lot of activity because the grandmother who owned the property helped to raise her grandkids. There was always something going on over there. In the EVPs, it sounds like a young black man talking since the neighbors next door were Afro-American. I'm only speculating that residual spiritual energy probably migrated to my mom's house from next door.

In the first session, there was this EVP where a young man said that Philip was over there, drunk.

195

Paranormal Investigations: The Cajun Ghost Hunter Chronicles

Spirit: Philip's over there drunk!

⌃: Philip's Drunk

In the next session, I was sitting on the floor with my back to the wall in the living room. On Saturday mornings when we were growing up, my siblings and I would have to clean the house while my mom would leave and go visit friends. Peter's job was to vacuum and mop the living room. I figured I would ask Mama if she wanted to have Peter use the old dust mop that I had found in her bedroom closet to clean the room. The answer surprised me and here's why!

My aunt Blondie had this motorized recliner at her house. She had become debilitated from strokes and had trouble moving around, so Uncle Lee had bought them this recliner that would lift the person sitting in it to a standing position so they could exit the chair without having to try to pull themselves out of it. The process is very, very slow and takes about a minute to get the sitting person to a standing position. It uses a scissor-jack principle and lifts the chair way up from horizontal to an almost-full vertical position to do it. This motor also makes the chair very heavy. Well, after my aunt died, somehow this chair ended up in the corner of the living room in my mom's house. I don't think the controls for the motor work any longer, and it was never used for that feature, only for sitting.

When I asked Mama if she wanted me to get Peter to dust mop the living room, I captured this voice that doesn't sound like a young black man. He said that he was in the damn chair and getting the slow motor! Was there a spirit attached to that motorized chair? What does he mean that he's getting the slow motor?

Stan: Mama, you want me to get Peter to dust mop the living room?
Spirit: I'm in the damn chair, getting the slow motor!

⌃: Getting the Slow Motor

Paranormal Investigations: The Cajun Ghost Hunter Chronicles

I then received this EVP that sounds like an elderly black woman saying that her feelings were hurt and not to play around there. Was this residual from the grandmother next door talking to one of her grandchildren?

Spirit: My feelings hurt! Don't play around here!

⌃: Don't Play around Here

The last session at my mom's house must be residual from next door. I captured two EVPs with one being the reverse speech of the other but related. In the forward speech, a spirit said that Billy hit Gram (Grandma). The reverse speech is related to the forward speech because the spirit said "Ow" and then said that he felt it, like he was the one that was hit.

Spirit: Billy hit Gram!
Spirit: Ow, I feel it!

⌃: Billy Hit Gram

XV

THE JOLET TOMB

http://www.cajunghosthunter.com/The_Jolet_Tomb.html

Whenever I went to Laurel Valley Plantation to record my sessions, I usually would stop at the Jolet Tomb, our family tomb, on the way. It is located on Menard Street in Thibodaux, Louisiana. I would go there on Saturday afternoons after Barbara left for work since I would have the latter part of the afternoon to capture my three-minute sessions at both places. I sometimes went there on Wednesdays during the summer after I attended my weekly mass at St. Joseph's Cathedral in Thibodaux, Louisiana. This is the same cemetery for the parishioners of the church. I don't know the history of how my grandfather Assie Jolet acquired the tomb. The people buried in it include my mother's grandmother Marie Leblanc Daigle; her second husband, Clemille Daigle; my mother's sister Odessa Jolet Daigle; her husband, Irving P. Daigle (son of Clemille); Hilda Jolet Wroblewski (my mother); Stanley Wroblewski (my father); and Paul Vacarro (husband of Peggy Daigle Vacarro, Aunt Odessa's daughter).

The tomb has four slots, two on top and two on the bottom, all above ground. Under the bottom two slots are the crypts where the bones of the dead relatives are placed and their caskets burned afterward in order to make room for the newly deceased relatives. It is specified in the perpetual care agreement with the caretakers that my grandmother Mabel Guillotte Jolet and my grandfather Assie J. Jolet always remain in the top two slots of the tomb.

Paranormal Investigations: The Cajun Ghost Hunter Chronicles

The Jolet family was very prestigious in the fifteenth century. In 1429, members of the family joined forces with Joan of Arc to fight the British at Orleans, France. On May 4, 1429, the battle began, and by May 8, Orleans had been taken by Joan's forces. The Battle of Patay on June 18, 1429, turned out to be the deciding factor in the Hundred Years' War, and after it, the dauphin of France, Charles VI, was escorted by Joan to Rheims for his coronation.

There is much history in the Jolet family. For instance, Louis Joliet was living with his family in Quebec, Canada, and studying to become a Jesuit priest when he met Father Jacques Marquette, originally born in France and commissioned by the governor of the region to survey the Mississippi River and teach religion to the Indians. They travelled all the way to Greenville, Mississippi, from the Great Lakes region and left packets of information at each Indian village so that in case anything happened to them, the next surveyor could pick them up. On their way back up north, Father Marquette and Louis had an accident in their canoe and lost all their supplies. They traveled back to Quebec and eventually returned to the Indian village near the site of the accident to retrieve the information that had been left there. When they returned to Quebec, Louis sent the papers to the king of France, who granted him a land grant on the Saint Lawrence Seaway, which is now an animal sanctuary 139 miles long by 40 miles wide. There is also a statue of Marquette and Joliet in a square in Chicago dedicated to their explorations and the night they slept in the woods at that location.

I started capturing credible EVPs from the tomb on June 18, 2011. I had gone to the tomb that afternoon and performed an FM scan. My father used to get off work on Thursday afternoons for a half day, and during the summertime, my brother Danny and I would lay out the crab nets and the hampers to have the supplies prepared to leave after lunch. In this EVP, I told my father that I had some crab nets and some melt (bait) and that we should go down Pointe Aux Chenes to catch some crabs. Instead of my father, I picked up this spirit voice with some interference in the middle of the exclamation that sounded exactly like my mother's voice telling me not to quit. I'm not sure exactly why

Paranormal Investigations: The Cajun Ghost Hunter Chronicles

she was telling me this. Perhaps it's because the whole family were quarreling with each other over the settlement of her estate and she wanted me to not quit loving my sister, Pat, who was the executor of the secession.

Stan: Got some crab net and the bait out and got some melt. Let's get in the car and go catch some crabs down Pointe Aux Chenes, OK?
Spirit: Oh, Stanley Junior, don't quit!

‸: Stanley Junior, Don't Quit

On June 25, 2011, I returned to the tomb after seeing Barbara off to work. Philip had gone freshwater fishing the day before, and I had cleaned up his catch of perch and fried them up for lunch. I started the FM session like I always do by putting my head up against the door of the tomb and telling my mother I was there. A spirit responded that Philip needed her.

Stan: Hello, Mama, it's Stanley Junior.
Spirit: Philip needs me!

‸: Philip Needs Me

I asked my mother where she was at lunchtime because I had some fried perch. She loved to eat fried perch when I was growing up, especially crunching on the tails after they were fried. A spirit responded that I was back. They recognized me and knew me now that I was visiting them on a regular basis.

Stan: Where were you at lunchtime? I was having me some fried perch!
Spirit: Stanley Junior's back!

‸: Stanley Junior's Back

Paranormal Investigations: The Cajun Ghost Hunter Chronicles

I went to the tomb on July 2, 2011, and performed another FM scan. I received two responses after I told my mom hello. The first one warmed my heart, and the second one was disturbing. The first response from a spirit told my mom, Hilda, that I loved her. The second response said that Stan was dead. I wondered if it was my mom telling me that my dad, Stanley Senior, was dead also.

Stan: Hello, Mama, it's Stanley Junior. Hello!?
Spirit: Hilda, he loves you!

⌃: Hilda, He Loves You

Stan: Hello, Mama, it's Stanley Junior. Hello!?
Spirit: Stan . . . dead!

⌃: Stan Dead

I asked my mom if she was happy in there with Daddy, and a spirit replied that I was back again.

Stan: Are you happy in there with Daddy?
Spirit: Stanley Junior's back!

⌃: Happy with Daddy

I returned to the Jolet tomb on July 9, 2011, and performed another FM scan. We had been having disputes within the family over my nephew, Randy, moving out of my mom's house so that we could sell it. He was having problems locating a new place to live, and arguments were occurring among my siblings and me. We had received word from Randy that he had found a place to live in Bayou Blue and that he would be moving soon.

When I told my mom that we might be getting Randy out of the house next month, I captured this angelic voice that told me that God heard

Paranormal Investigations: The Cajun Ghost Hunter Chronicles

the subject and for us to make more love. I found that statement so profound and captivating!

Stan: We might finally get Randy out your house next month!
Spirit: God heard subject! Let's make more love!

︿: Let's Make More Love

As I was preparing to leave, I asked the spirits if there was anything they wanted to tell me. A spirit said that I was her Stanley and that she loved me.

Stan: Is there anything you want to tell me before I leave? Anybody?
Spirit: Hi Stanley, I love you!

︿: Hi Stanley

I went to the tomb on July 23, 2011, and performed an FM scan. As you can see from the dates that I'm posting, I was visiting the tomb weekly. This was my last visit until after my Las Vegas vacation at the end of the month. I captured one very prolific message during this session telling me that Jesus Christ will come. Was this residual from one of the priests buried in the cemetery?

Spirit: Jesus Christ will come!

︿: Jesus Christ Will Come

After my vacation, I finally made it back to the tomb on August 20, 2011. I performed an ambient EVP session with no FM scan. It was late in the evening, and you can hear cicadas singing in the background noise. In the first EVP that I captured, I heard this spirit that sounded like my mother. My aunt Blondie (Althea Jolet Duet) had suffered a series of strokes, and at one point in time, my mom was her power of attorney. So it was appropriate that I would hear this spirit in this EVP say that they were talking for Blondie.

Paranormal Investigations: The Cajun Ghost Hunter Chronicles

Spirit: I'm talking for Blondie!

︿: I'm Talking for Blondie

I next received these spirits telling me that I seem gay and that I sleep around!

Spirit One: You seem gay!
Spirit Two: You sleep around!

︿: You Seem Gay

At the end of this EVP session, I had my head resting against the nameplate on the front of the tomb when I picked up these creepy, disembodied howls that seemed to emanate from the tomb. When I processed this session and heard these howls, it reminded me of the mythological three-headed dog, Cerberus, guarding the gates of the underworld so that wandering souls could not escape.

︿: Disembodied Howls

On October 29, 2011, I had made arrangements with my sister, Patricia "Pat" Beacom, to go to the tomb to place some flowers for our relatives and parents since All Saints' Day on November 1, 2011, was forthcoming. I brought my equipment with me and figured that with Pat there, we could capture some good EVPs. Pat and I used to take turns bringing my parents their groceries on Saturdays when they were both alive. After my mother broke her hip and was placed in a nursing home, we would take turns tending to my mother's needs. Pat was my mother's power of attorney and executor of the estate, so she had to give more of her time caring for her in the nursing home. For that, I am forever grateful.

I had started an FM scan EVP session when Pat went up to the nameplate, knocked, and asked if anyone was home. A spirit replied that they were home!

206

Paranormal Investigations: The Cajun Ghost Hunter Chronicles

Pat: Is anybody home?
Spirit: They home!

△: They Home

A minute later when I asked my mother to tell her daughter that she loved her, a spirit graciously replied that Hilda loved Patricia. How intelligent and responsive! Was this my mother directly answering? Instead of saying "I," the spirit said "Hilda," so was she identifying who was speaking?

Stan: Mama, tell your daughter you love her!
Spirit: Hilda love Patricia!

△: Hilda Love Patricia

I captured this final EVP in the session. I was telling Pat how the spirits talk about Philip at my house all the time, and a spirit can be heard saying that it was their favorite ghost house.

Stan: They talk about Philip at my house.
Pat: What?
Spirit: My favorite ghost house!

△: My Favorite Ghost House

I visited the tomb on December 17, 2011, and performed an FM scan. I captured one quality EVP from a female spirit. After I told my mother I was there, the spirit said for me to get her paper. This may have been my mother. Sometimes when I went to her house, as I was opening the door, she would tell me from her rocker to go get her newspaper that would be either in her driveway or her yard.

Stan: Hello, Mama, it's Stanley Junior.
Spirit: Get my paper, Junior.

Paranormal Investigations: The Cajun Ghost Hunter Chronicles

⌒: Get My Paper

My visits to the tomb became less frequent in 2012. Since I was contacting spirits at other sites and capturing quality evidence, there wasn't any reason to continue trying to contact the dead at my parents' tomb. I went to the tomb on March 12, 2012, and captured one FM scan EVP where a spirit asked me how Philip was doing.

Spirit: How's Philip?

⌒: How's Philip?

Harold and I went to the tomb on October 28, 2012. Although we have perpetual care for the tomb, it is still the practice of Catholics to go the graves of their loved ones prior to Halloween and paint the grave sites in preparation for All Saints' Day on November 1. Since Harold is a professional painter, we hired him to perform this task annually, and this was his first time doing it. I went with him to show him where it was located and to assist. Of course, I had to perform some EVPs while we completed our task.

In the first FM session, I asked my mother if she knew Harold's name as he was painting behind the cross on top of the tomb. A spirit responded correctly, saying both his first and last name.

Stan: That's Barbara's brother back there. You know his name?
Spirit: That's Harold Chauvin!

⌒: That's Harold Chauvin

I then received this EVP from a spirit that said "Aunt Blondie." I have previously described my mother's affection for her sister Blondie, and perhaps this was Mama calling out to her.

Spirit: Aunt Blondie!

Paranormal Investigations: The Cajun Ghost Hunter Chronicles

‿: Aunt Blondie

For the final FM scan EVP, I asked my mom if she would like some pizza. A spirit replied that they would like a great big slice.

Stan: Would you like some pizza?
Spirit: Great big slice!

‿: Great Big Slice

I performed an ambient EVP session while Harold was painting on top of the tomb. I picked up a couple of EVPs. The first one was a spirit who told me to "pray for Mommy."

Spirit: Pray for Mommy!

‿: Pray for Mommy

The last EVP that I captured and published for this book finalizes my research and presentation of my data. A spirit said that they could hear my voice. How appropriate because now, I can hear them too!

Spirit: We can hear a voice!

‿: We Can Hear A Voice

XVI

PARANORMAL INVESTIGATIONS: EPILOGUE

The Cajun Ghost Hunter Chronicles

*Lord I am not worthy that you should enter under my roof,
but only say the Word and my soul shall be healed!*

—Matthew 8:5–8

This concludes my presentation of the evidence I gathered over a two-year period with my instruments. I can't explain precisely where these voices that you hear originate since no one has ever come back from the dead to describe what they have truly witnessed or who they have met after crossing over for a period of time. Yes, there are some people that have had near-death or out-of-body experiences, but not for a long period of time such that months or years have passed. Some people think that these voices are aliens that are speaking over the radio frequencies or projecting human voices into the ambient recordings.

I believe that spirits are people that previously existed on this earth and they are now with us all the time. I think that at historical sites, the grief and tribulations that the spirits have suffered while alive are relived over and over, as depicted in the residual recordings I have captured. I have presented many instances, especially in Laurel Valley, where residual voices expressed their thoughts about events that happened in their daily lives.

The truly amazing data, though, shows that there are spirits that are intelligent and can respond and interact with this real world, giving correct answers to questions that only they would have known the answers when alive. The case with Barbara's father, Gordon, correcting me about the origin of the Pietà and whose casket it belonged is evidence that spirits can not only give intelligent answers, they also can correct the living when we have made mistakes. This was one

Paranormal Investigations: The Cajun Ghost Hunter Chronicles

of my epiphanies! Perhaps they have the ability to summon enough energy to use physical force to help us when we use poor judgment and place ourselves in dangerous situations and make things in this physical world move, thus keeping us out of harm's way.

Maybe that is why people think that miracles occur—because our loved ones are keeping a watchful eye over us and helping us in our daily lives. They could be the angels that have been recorded throughout history as helping people and nations in their hours of need. For example, maybe Joan of Arc had the gift of hearing spirit voices without using an EVP recorder and these spirits gave her intelligent advice on how to defeat the English at Patay so that Charles VI could be crowned king of France. Was this really a case of divine intervention or spirit manipulation? Maybe it's a little of both happening at the same time!

I mentioned at the beginning of this book that as a metals chemist, I can't see the processes as they occur at the atomic level and have to rely on the measurements recorded from the instruments that I use. Likewise, in communicating with spirits, I can't see the ethereal beings that are talking to me. I can only rely on the voices from the evidence that I collect using the instruments that I have available. The similarity between the two methods is that data are gathered from instruments to give information from the unseen world around us. The only difference is that step five, demonstrating the validity and reproducibility of a hypothesis by using the scientific method, cannot be verified in the paranormal realm.

This is why I stated in the prologue that this is one individual's personal spiritual journey, namely mine. Anyone can purchase these instruments online for a reasonable cost and download the same software that I use to speak to their loved ones and communicate with the dead. The only hindrances to anyone wanting this ability to communicate with those that have passed are their religious and philosophical beliefs.

214

Paranormal Investigations: The Cajun Ghost Hunter Chronicles

Because of my upbringing and my education, I have had to reevaluate both of these subjects and have come to this realization. I no longer need faith because faith is the acceptance of the teachings of a religion that an unseen deity exists, whether it be Catholicism, Buddhism, or Islam. My experiences have shown me that not only does this deity exist but also that there is something else beyond this life where we live and breathe. There is a place where our loved ones go, and for some reason, some of them can still reach out to us in this world without needing access to their corporeal bodies.

I now pray for redemption. Because of my past upbringing here in the Catholic culture of South Louisiana, I am comfortable going to a church representing the religion I was taught. The church that I go to is really not that important because I know now that when I achieve that state of prayer where I feel that I am talking to my deity—whether his name is God, Buddha, or Allah—that if I listen real hard, he may talk back! The day that I do cross over, I hope that He will have heard my requests and allow me to go to that place where my loved ones have called out to me and are now waiting.

I have more evidence that I have been collecting that is so compelling that I will have to write about it in the sequels to this book. I have stories of people that have been killed only to come back and talk to their loved ones in the most unheard-of places hundreds of miles from where they passed. I have been to haunted houses where I not only captured spirit voices on my instruments, I also actually heard them with my own ears and simultaneously captured the voices on my digital camera! However, these are stories that will be added to my sequels of *The Cajun Ghost Hunter Chronicles.*

XVII

BIBLIOGRAPHY

1. Christine Word, <u>Ghosts Along the Bayou</u>, "T-Frere's Amelie," 102–110; "Mysteries at Jefferson Island," 59–68, 1988.
2. ^: Troy Taylor, "Mistress of Death: The Haunted History of Madame Lalaurie," 2000.
3. Jill Pascoe, <u>Louisiana's Haunted Plantations, "Woodland Plantation,"</u> 129–138, 2004.
4. ^: Woodland Plantation and Spirits Hall, "History," 2013.
5. ^: <u>Lindsay & Dickey History, Bradish Johnson, 2008.</u>
6. ^: <u>Rip Van Winkle Gardens, Jefferson Island</u>, "History," 2009.
7. ^: <u>Explore the History and Culture of Southeastern Louisiana,</u> "Madewood."
8. ^: <u>National Trust for Historic Preservation</u>, "Rebuilding Madewood" by Wayne Curtis, May/June 2010.
9. ^: <u>Briscoe Center for American History, the University of Texas at Austin</u>, "A Guide to the Pugh Family Papers, 1807–1907," 2009–2011.
10. ^: <u>"Descendants of *Father of Francis Pugh 'Glendover Hall' Pugh,"</u> "Generation No.7, 17. Thomas Whitmell Pugh," 7.
11. ^: <u>Hauntings</u>, "The Hauntings of Laurel Valley Plantation," 2011.
12. ^: <u>Laurel Valley Plantation: An American History Blackboard.</u>

Paranormal Investigations: The Cajun Ghost Hunter Chronicles

13. ^: Daily Comet.com, Lafourche Parish, Louisiana, "Ghosts Haunts Mostly the Imagination, Plantation Owners Say" by Nikki Buskey, October 31, 2007.
14. ^: Debbie S. Terry, "Laurel Valley Plantation," 2009.
15. ^: Wikipedia, "Bonnie Springs Ranch," February 2012.
16. ^: Lynn Sutherland Olsen's Paranormal TV Blog, "Ghost Adventures: 'La Palazza,'" November 13, 2010.
17. ^: China Ranch Date Farm, "History," 2013.
18. ^: Welcome to Friends of the Fort, "History," 2013.
19. ^: The Las Vegas Review-Journal, "Helen Stewart" by K. J. Evans, February 7, 1999.
20. ^: Jamaica National Heritage Trust, "St. Mary's Anglican," 2011.
21. Historical plaque in front of Conch Shell House, 492 North Sound Road, Georgetown, Grand Cayman.
22. ^: Wikipedia, "Wreck of the Ten Sail," 2003.
23. ^: Pedro St. James National Historic Site, Cayman Islands, "Great House," 2013.
24. Pictures of Helen Stewart are from the UNLV Libraries Special Collections, 2013.